Nondual Passion

A Quality of Consciousness in
Nondual Therapy

Georgi Y. Johnson

VeReCreations

◎

Published by VeReCreations

Paperback: ISBN 978-1-912517-09-1

Ingram Spark Edition

Cover design: Austen Rubben

Cover image is adapted from a photo of the original work within the series
"Europe a Prophecy" by William Blake, The British Museum. Asset
number 38787001. Copy D, plate 1, frontispiece: "The Ancient of Days"; a
bearded nude male (probably Urizen) crouching in a heavenly sphere, its
light partially covered by clouds; his left arm holding a pair of compasses
and reaching down with them, measuring the surrounding darkness.
1794. All interior images are from self-generated infograms or adapted
from artwork of the poet William Blake from the public domain.

Dedication

For my father, Tony Johnson (1942-1981).

You were a blazing comet that burned bright and vanquished into a legacy of infinite potential.

Thank you for my life.

Thank you that sleepless evening when you lifted me in your arms and showed me that if we gaze into the dark night for long enough, then many stars appear.

May you be forever passionate.

"To see a world in a grain of sand
And a heaven in a wild flower,
Hold infinity in the palm of your hand
And eternity in an hour."

WILLIAM BLAKE

Passion (n.) c. 1200, from Late Latin Passionem (nominative passio)
"suffering, enduring," from past-participle stem of Latin pati "to
endure, undergo, experience..."

TABLE OF CONTENTS

PROLOGUE

Cry me a river

"The water you touch in a river is the last of that which has passed, and the first of that which is coming. Thus it is with time present."

LEONARDO DA VINCI

Between the entrancing vibrations of our thinking mind and the robust fact of our physical body, there is a river – the river of pure experience. This river runs between our ideas and our actuality. It flows between our imagination and our reality. Its torrents cascade through the cracks between silence and sensation, between the inner darkness and the sensual arousal. Its currents move between our attitudes, habits and reflexes, and our genes – those minute templates that filter our physical presence in the here and now.

Nondual Passion

Like all rivers, this river of experience is in constant flux. It rolls and winds, unique in each snapshot of form. Its rippling surfaces reflect patterns of light and shadow, glinting in sacred converse with the sky above. At the same time, its undercurrents can be slower, more powerful, and pulled by deeper forces.

It is in this river of experience that we find ourselves alive. It is through rivers of feeling that we consciously awaken, and the deeper we delve into this river of life, the deeper life comes to us.

What is a thought, a fact, or an imagination, but the experience of mental movement? What is a yearning, an emotion, or a depth of feeling, but the experience of that flow of sentient impressions? What is physical sensation, sight, sound, touch, taste, or smell, but the running experience of sensory information?

All that we could ever think ourselves to be, all the memory accumulating through us, and all we could ever imagine ourselves to be – all this is alive as the river of experience in the here and now.

The river is a changing, turning, evolution of impressions of who we are, what we are and where we are. Yet just as it defines us, the river can itself only be defined by its perpetual movement. It never stops moving, yet, seen from far above, it is perfectly still.

The river of experience flows with the vast paradoxes of creation. Unchanging, it never stays the same. Changing constantly, it is timeless. Indestructible, it dies in every moment. Ungraspable, it sustains all life. Undeniable, it willows each definition into the equanimous stream of its perpetual unfolding.

All knowledge, no matter how evident, hard-won, proven, attested and scientific, has arisen through this river of experience, and it is only through experience of the fact that the fact continues to live. Without the river of experience, all knowledge is an un-watered desert of decaying thought.

This river of life even touches us in the hollow spaces, running underground, through remote caves and within mountains. Even the lack of life is an experience. Even negation, absence, falsity, and the lie can only appear as twists and spirals within the ongoing movement of the river of life. From the supreme creator, through to our worldly authorities, oracles, conspiracy theorists and the dictatorship of collective mind - all are but fluid forms in the river of varying sensation, turning, reflecting, and undulating as one inseparable, multidimensional spiral of life. All arise in sensation, through experience, as experience, out of experience. Even where tides compete and the vortex appears, the river rises as cyclones of steam.

The work of mind, the play of the body, and the grace of the heart merge and unify within the river of experience. Even the sense of separation and split flows there, undivided from the whole cosmic circulation of water through ice, fluid, and cloud.

What is experience? What is this unifying source in which body, heart, mind, inside, outside, self, and other flow as one elemental manifestation of all that we are? How to navigate this river, and who would be the navigator?

Each waterdrop in the river is a moment of consciousness. In that timeless moment, there is a confluence of past and future in the now. In that one drop of water, subject and object merge as one happening. The perceiver is one with the perceived and the seer is one with the seen. Here, there is the love story of life occurring within the push and pull of oneness and endless variation. This conscious moment can be at once a single drop, and at the entire universal ocean of life.

Yet there is depth to the momentous. Within the unity there is a vibrational quality in which experience is flavored with subtler resonance. This tear drop can be alive with the atmosphere of pain, the next with joy, the other with the succulence of physical yearning, and the next with the frustration of vital force. This resonance structures how one molecule dances with the next. It is inseparable from a morphic mist of quality in which each atmosphere is wondrously unique, essentially immeasurable, and incomparable.

Some atmospheres are full of yearning, reaching into the ether toward completion. Others are unwell, sorrowfully falling back to stardust. Here there is a sacred rhythm of destruction, chaos and reformation, serving momentum to the healing currents of creation.

Subtler still, there are atmospheres that are instantly rewarded, alive with harmony and the fulfilment of pure becoming. These are alive in the subtle potency of well-being and yet are expanding in formless unity. Unaltered by collisions with greater density, they gracefully move through empty spaces, around, within, before and behind each moment of becoming.

These atmospheres are the mists hovering over bodies of water, at the threshold of transformation. They are also the of softness that lives within each molecule of water, humming melodies of true nature, resonating formulas of being and infiltrating every particle of form. These moods, states, mists and skyscapes are found in the space between and around electrons, brushing the membranes of molecules and spiraling through the epicenter of the biochemical bond. They emanate from and return to the ungraspable sky of awareness.

When we sense our loneliness, we are that awareness out of which that loneliness sounds. As loneliness enters our blood, our muscles, and our bones, we become that ache of loneliness, which arises within that forever pure awareness - like a question. It is question about belonging, about reunion, about purpose, about passion, about coming home and about becoming the home we never left. Out of awareness our consciousness sprouts and touches the area of pain, blessing it with memory - the memory of what this fracture of experience truly is. The touch of consciousness awakens the sense of belonging within the sense of separation. It awakens connection within the isolation. And often, easily, in this way, a crunch of pain becomes a touch of bliss, as the river of experience flows on.

The currents of the river move with formulas of creation, of transformation, evolution, and of manifestation. Just as every inch of form reaches toward the light, we naturally turn toward our true nature. We turn toward it, through it, reflecting its infinity, dancing in its joy.

From great heights we have dived into the river of life. We have felt her freshness and changeability, her newness, and her antiquity. We have tasted her moments and we have bathed in the waters of her being. We have travelled within the moment of the single molecule to the charge of vitality and its mists of emotion. Here, intoxicated by the perfume of nascent beauty we have fallen through the crevices of conscious control. Within that enticing resonance, we suddenly, penitently know ourselves as an unadulterated awareness, boundlessly existing through all the empty spaces – even within the emptiness of the densest bodies of form.

And yet, within that single, individual drop, the facilitator of the vast universal ocean of life, there is more. The journey perpetually begins.

Deep within the river of life, not beneath, behind, or above, not underpinning or transcending, but within, there is the sublime mystery of all that we are. Ubiquitous and so subtle that we might call it empty.

This is the perennial, indivisible space existing through and between all currents of sensation. This is the space that allows all variation and speed. Prior to awareness, we are identical, everything and nothing, being and non-being, neither light nor dark, neither subject nor object, Not I, Not Other than I [1].

We are that which allows the ecstatic reunion of life with itself. We are the area through which touch occurs and so we are facilitators of bliss. We are the source of all perception and here, where we perceive ourselves reflected through apparitions of beauty, we wonder at the revelation from inside out. Without this self-identical space of infinite and eternal singularity, without this wellspring of self, no passage of experience could occur, and the river could not flow. We are the secret mystery and wonder of the river.

At the core of all matter there is this rhythmic impulse through which the hidden becomes seen. Its command, rippling through all the rivers of the universe is to "be", to manifest, to elucidate the melody of the living. In resisting this command of being, we suffer, and we lose our way. These are sad corners of the river, where experience slows – for a while. In moving with the command of being, we arise with universal power, unique within the manifold field of unity.

In that spontaneous arising, in the release of form, we are spotlessly received. All moments of the river, from its newborn reflections, through swamplands to subterranean passages of darkness, are received as living impressions and expressions of home.

And here is the river of life flowing through all worlds, charged with the vast mysteries of perceptive emptiness, the living core of all we are. Here is the command and the fulfillment; the release of life, and the choiceless reward; the question and the answer; the unknown and the knowing; the confusion and meaning; the insentience and sensing; the purpose and the passion.

The river of life flows through degrees of light, a conscious, aware, emptiness spiraling through space that is always easily found, intimately, in this tender, naked, scarcely earthed moment of your unique becoming. Guided by wellness through paths of least resistance, the passion insists on the revelation of the river, the awesome, sustaining, perpetual cascade into wholeness.

This is the solemn prayer of this work: to show you some of the majesty of all you are, that together in unity, we will unfold through this journey some of the passion – the turbulence of the living miracle – that timelessly waits to awaken through us in this - at once sublime and yet radically human - moment of divinity.

Nondual Passion

INTRODUCTION: NONDUAL THERAPY

The true nature of healing

"Be passionately dispassionate - that is all."

SRI NISARGADATTA MAHARAJ

Who am I? What am I? Where am I? What am I here for? What is the point? What is the purpose of life? Why do I exist? All of us, without exception - whether through strife or through life, through pain or gain, through longing or wronging, through wisdom or schism – all of us will come to these pulsing questions asked with insistence by our existence: Who is this? What is this? Where is this? Who am I? What am I? Where am I?

These are the questions of poets, scientists, engineers, philosophers, innovators, artists, priests, mystics, and sages. They are timeless because they are sourced outside of time. They are boundless because they are asked into an infinite space of the unknown. They are fiery questions, lighting up beacons of curiosity, as each answer ignites another question. They are formless, because the questioner is life itself, before any differentiation, into shape, size, or frequency.

Therapy without conditions

Life is asking the question of anything we could imagine ourselves to be. Yet our imagination is limited by fearful anticipations based on depressed conclusions. These existential questions, even without answers, reveal the forgotten vistas of endless potential. They endow meaning, purpose and evolutionary momentum. They transmit wonder, awe and curiosity. They put light on old battle lines, revealing the false claim within every limitation – that this line drawn in the sand long ago marks the end of the world. Suffused with the sense of impossibility, these limits claim to be impassable, that there is an end to being, and that there our true nature is restricted. In short, that we are stuck. Questions can dispel this illusion of limitation, by asking with a naughtiness: is this really true? What is on the other side of this so-called battle line?

As consciousness awakens with open eyes to the living body of earth, it might look for partitions of cities, states, and nations. It might look for the divisions in color, creed, and species. It might seek the tyrannical rift between man and woman. Yet it will not see black and white, but a myriad colors. It will see bodies of water and gradations of mountains, moving clouds and the awesome suspension of the planet in stillness, just as she turns on her axis while journeying through her orbit of intergalactic belonging. It will see unlimited beauty through variety within wholeness and it will see that it is good.

We look for limitations to define us, but where we put our faith in these limits, hoping that restriction will somehow keep us safe, we are always horribly, thankfully betrayed. This is because the consciousness that we are cannot be controlled, contained, conspired, or condemned. We are the conscious life before, beyond and after all limitations have passed. Limitations fail us and we find ourselves falling into the formless emptiness of boundless unborn potential. When our world of restriction ends, we find that we are free. In Nondual Therapy, this self-realization of the limitless within form happens safely, by degrees, sentient fiber by sentient fiber.

So, it is with our nominal identity, and the ideas we have about our shape, size, weight, status, and destiny. None of these can truly define us. Consciousness has the power to blow such suppositions apart, as if they never were. Consciousness will shed illusions and shatter the notions that have stressed the spirit, depressed the heart, and numbed the living body. Consciousness is the alpha and omega of all healing processes.

How is it that what seems like destruction, devastation and disintegration can lead to expansion, release and a lightness of being? How is it that our greatest suffering - the dread of the end of our world - when unmasked, can seem like nothing more than a bad joke told in a grainy way?

And-and

It can be thus because of a shivering possibility: that we are far more magnificent, powerful, and brimming with potential than we ever dared imagine. We are our own creators and the architects of our own destruction within a multisensual narrative in which we are the one inspiration. The whole universe is centering in us and swirling in a sensuous storm around the core of our individual doorway of consciousness: the doorway we call "I".

Throughout the ages, the focus of sages has been on the evolution from the judgmental, discriminating mind, to the dimension of wisdom. The judgmental mind is caught in polarity. It splits experience into good and bad, wanted, and unwanted, light and darkness, winners, and losers. In this splitting of reality into twos, it creates localized energetic battlefields of comparison, competition, and conflict. Out of this warzone of consensual conflict, it appoints a commander in chief – a dictator of reality to which all thoughts must conform. This commander is often the loudest voice of the collective mind. Already wounded and condemned by eons of perpetual warfare, he is paranoid and feels constantly victimized. He speaks the language of fear and threat. His fuel is the rage at injustice. His mandate is to bring peace, and to do this, he wages perpetual war.

Nondual wisdom moves beyond this nonsensical belief in the division into two, ultimately separated, mutually exclusive sides of a conflict that are engaged in an existential war. It releases our consciousness out of the causeless struggle found in the either-or, into the self-evident truth of "both". It is not me or you, it is both of us. You cannot have a choice without at least two options. Even after you decide on one option, the both still are here. It is not *either-or*, it is both. It is not you or me, it is us, together. This is a factual wisdom hidden in plain sight.

In the "and-and" – we find the interdependent nature of all things. There is no light except as a measure of darkness; no mother without a father; no parents without a child; no left without right; no up without down; no rising without falling; no winning without losing; no good without bad; no pleasure without pain; no death without birth; no me without you; no self without other.

They say it takes two to tango. In our physical dimension this is true. Without duality, there would be no flow of love, no bliss of touch, no peace of togetherness, no movement, and no life. The split into two creates the bliss of experience through friction. If we were not separate, we could not rejoice in one another. If we were not one, we also would not rejoice in one another. All experience is a sensuous celebration of separation within unity.

War zones

The illusion is not in the dance of duality, but in the belief that this tango is an existential fight to the death – to the annihilation of one side OR the other. This either-or belief states that the universe is not big enough for the two of us, and that only one of us can come out a winner. It's true. We are really, collectively believing in this absurdity – investing all our vitality in the destruction of each other, which is our own self destruction.

Yet self-destruction is an impossibility because the belief in duality is the belief in impossibility. It is illusory. If I am self-destructing, which one of me is destroying which one of me? Which one lives, which one dies? You got it: everyone dies. It's inseparable. The wellbeing of each part is inseparable from the whole.

Formed out of the toxic waste of fear, the illusions of either-or thinking are ungrounded and unearthed. They are in conflict with direct observation. My right hand does not compete with my left hand. My right foot is not out to kill my left foot. If you are bad it doesn't make me good. My future is not at war with my past. If the world is evil, it doesn't mean that I'm an angel. Although I could be an angel dressed as a demon in an evil world.

Fear of pain is intoxicating, and it compels our consciousness into beliefs based on death, negation, and existential erasure, as if we could uncreate what has already happened. As if we could undo time or erase a pain that is already felt. We believe we can "get rid" of parts of who we are, not just from the present and future, but also from memory. And because we cannot do this, we pretend that we can by smothering it with the insentient energy of ignorance and denial.

When we are determined to get rid of a part of ourselves, we need to deeply believe in that part as being definitive of who and what we are. We religiously pay deference to the offensive part. In a way, we enslave ourselves to the suffering we fear. We make it the big issue. We make it matter as that one part which has the power to disturb our universal peace, disrupt our god-given vitality, and distract our cosmic consciousness. The very strength of our self-rejection brings an energetic charge to that which we are trying to reject. We pile the pain of rejection on the pain of rejection on the pain of rejection. There is no wonder that what we resist, persists, with bells on it. The force of our aversion brings force to the whole field of aversion, until all we feel is aversion, until it gets so horrible that we don't want to feel anything anymore at all.

This is where nonduality becomes Nondual Therapy, through the tremendous power of truthfulness in accepting all experience, even the vibratory cruelty of the energy of negation, within the field of shared conscious inquiry.

We cannot get rid of what has passed, but we can change our attitude to it, expand our range of perspectives on it and deepen our insight into it. Healing does not happen through the elimination of parts of the psyche, it happens through the transformative power of inclusivity. Therapy is not a violence, but a shared process of softening, opening, and safe revelation. It is a process of relaxation into awareness. In every healing process, we move from disease to a fluctuating unease, to a sense of unconditional ease where we even begin to forget what we were fighting for.

To be well

This is the paradigm shift of Nondual Therapy – from a dimension of conflict to one of inclusion and overview. From core contraction of time and space where freedom appears to be loss, to the self-realization that regardless of contraction, freedom can never be lost.

The truth will set us free, and this wisdom has clinical applications that can turn a conventional therapy room into an opportunity for uncensored Satsang, and unparalleled depth healing within an atmosphere of compassion.

In Nondual Therapy, this liberating truth is not a "thing" or a fact from the world of "things". It is the sense of truth, of atmosphere, vibration, or intuition, that moves through the skin, blood, gut, and bones of us.

Nondual Passion

Truth is one of the deeper senses of consciousness that will guide us into the core of our own being, through the halls of shame and the old gates of loneliness horrified by the prison walls of isolation. It will lead us out of the whole territory of stress and danger and into the dimension of true nature, the Garden of Eden which is the dimension of our unfettered, living consciousness.

This dance of duality is not doomed to be an eternal, existential slavery, but is an evolutionary passage of passion in which we unfold, by degrees of sustainability, into purer expressions of source. We are hardwired for this direction; programmed for passion; and coded for bliss. Every moment of our existence through varied densities of form is reaching toward this fulfilment.

Imagine or remember a new-born baby. When the baby cries, it is out of need, a need to return to wellbeing. This quality of wellbeing includes qualities of peace, connection, relaxation, fulfilment, and care. Even the baby's pain reaches toward wellbeing – or "being well".

Adverse experiences are literally vibratory encounters between our naturalness and the confused and unresolved energies in the environment. There is a shock of dissonance or disharmony. When there is a loss of balance or energetic bewilderment, we seek balance and clarity. Our whole being tends toward the harmony of wellbeing through all expressions of form – physical, emotional, and mental. This process of refinement into higher harmony is evolutionary. It is part of our deeper intention and manifest purpose in being here in freedom.

When we are shocked in our naturalness, or wounded in our living responsiveness, there is a reflex to pull back. Expanding energy contracts. These contractions aim to protect against further assault. They seek to numb the pain of the next blow. They shield us from the outer world and seek to disable that which has been unsafe. We instinctively seek coping strategies through trying to find the cause of the horrible discomfort of contraction. Condoned by the environment, we often end up blaming that exact experience in which we were shocked.

For example, when we were mocked because we were innocent – we blame the innocence of true nature for the mockery. When we are shamed in our purity, we blame the purity for the shaming. When we got into trouble because we were free – we blame the freedom for the trouble. In all, we are conditioned to blame our true nature for our suffering. The vibration of consciousness gets energetically associated with the vibration of pain, and as a result, we disconnect still more from our naturalness, which causes still more suffering.

Part of the effect of contraction is that we lose freedom of movement. The flow of quality energy gets frozen. Vitality gets reduced, and we lose grace and naturalness. In the density of contraction (contracted purity, for example), this frozen energy is denied time, space, and movement, yet it now reverberates with layers of suffering. The pain is not functional, so we numb it, by withdrawing consciousness. At first it is an occasional pain when we are triggered. In time, and without attention, the state of contraction gets fixed. It appears as part of normality, as something that has always been there, that will never go away. At this stage, the very notion of a nondual quality, like purity for example, can seem conceptual. Purity cannot "be" in the real world. Purity is a fantasy of fools; it's an impure world.

Nondual Qualities

Natural & spontaneous.

Evolutionary.

Eternal and infinite.

Sensory.

One with conscious awareness.

Conduits of harmony and wellbeing.

Yet our consciousness is pure. It is made of purity. When we become conscious of the energy of our shame, we begin to experience it in purity. We begin to reverse the process of contraction. Rather than feeling ashamed in our purity, we begin to feel the purity of our shame. As we realize the purity within

34

that field of resonance, and the pure space within the physiology of the emotion, the shame has freedom to move again. It de-contracts, de-freezes and reunites with the undifferentiated purity within conscious awareness. Decontraction releases vitality, as voltage that has been short wired now becomes available to the whole. A healing momentum builds up.

It is no big news that love restores wellbeing, or that peace brings ease and relaxation. It is not rocket science that the energy of freedom brings solace when we feel trapped, or that the energy of joy uplifts a grieving heart. If beauty did not have a tremendous healing impact, then we would not flock in our free time to museums and places with awesome views. If the sense of connection was optional, we would not be dying from loneliness while the world turns its face.

The qualities of our true nature are not optional by-products of increased functionality or the latest medication. They are foundational to all wellbeing. They are the most abundant healing resource in the universe, and they are free, unlimited, and directly accessible to every living being. They are accessible as the qualities of consciousness, and wherever we are conscious, there they will be, whispering to us to be well. It is out of these ageless insights into the fundamentally transformative, evolutionary, and healing nature of consciousness that Nondual Therapy is emerging.

A nondual calling

Nondual Therapy acknowledges and harnesses this natural tendency toward well-being, whether it is physical, emotional, or mental. This is felt as a yearning toward the qualities of true nature. It is as if those qualities at the source ourselves are reaching toward those qualities in the whole. There is no private fulfillment. When we touch the quality inside ourselves, our whole drive is to share it with others. When we lose the connection inside ourselves, we call for it, like a teardrop resonating with the ocean.

When we realize the transient, sensory nature of separation, division, and discrimination, we begin to expand as conscious awareness. This is the very field in which all sensory vibration occurs, including the sense of division. There is a plain-sight, self-evident inclusivity of all phenomena in the here and now and there is boundless peace. These phenomena – physical sensations, feelings, emotions, and thoughts – are of a vibratory nature, arising and evaporating within our feeling awareness.

Healing depends on three principles: time, space, and movement. When these three are liberated through the realization that we are the eternal, spacious awareness in which the movement occurs, the whole field begins to vibrate with greater harmony and wellbeing.

In this, Nondual Therapy is deeply holistic, treating mind, emotional state, and body within one field of awareness. All impressions arise as experience, which is inseparable from this pure awareness. In its original meaning, the word "therapy" means to make whole. Nondual Therapy recruits and resources a wholeness beyond all the old coding of pain. It ventures a wholeness which is not a creation, but a recovery of the pure wellbeing of who we are, and who we will always be, irrespective of any play of experience.

Our true nature mediates the three worlds of universal consciousness, self-consciousness, and the collective unconscious. In this, Nondual Therapy is a resource, directed at the source of all we are in the infinite here and the eternal now. It resources through direct experience, to the core of experience, and from here to the spontaneous true nature of conscious awareness. It works with life, as life, in life.

Nondual qualities or the qualities of our true nature are often misconceived, reduced to a state of competition with negative emotions, and replaced by structures of ethical obligation. Nondual qualities are not primarily behaviors but are spontaneously arising vibrations, with an evolutionary purpose. They are unconditional, unlimited by time and space, meaning they are timeless and boundless. They are abundant, in infinite supply. They do not run out, and they never get lost. They cannot be injured or taken away.

Contractions

Need time and space.

Claim autonomy from the whole.

Express through the "either-or".

Have reduced sense and sensitivity.

Conceal living energy trapped in the past.

Become normative states.

Seek protection from pain.

Heal through Consciousness.

Each nondual quality is accessed through our sensory ability. We feel them. We have a sense of truth, for example, or we able to sense love, peace, or freedom. The sensing of the quality invites it. In this, each nondual quality is an entry to the whole of true nature. As our sensory ability arises out of sensory awareness, the vibrations of nondual qualities are inseparable from awareness. Another way to say this is that they are the refined, vibratory nature of awareness.

The transformational effect of nondual qualities is that they pull form toward greater balance and harmony, orienting the mind, body, and heart toward increasing degrees of wellbeing. This brings release, reward, rejuvenation, and resource, often accompanied by a liberation of consciousness. Nondual qualities are both awakened by the touch of consciousness and deliver a liberation of consciousness.

When nondual qualities contract, through the process of shocks in manifestation through greater densities of vibration, there is a lack of time and space. There is a splitting of consciousness between the dominant perspective, and the contracted one. Contraction is a protective reflex, a resistance, and in this, time and space are withdrawn. However, some consciousness remains within the contracted form, and this claims its own perspective.

Because contractions are a split in consciousness born of conflict with an area of experience, they are reflected in either-or thinking, or binary mind. This polarization reduces feeling sensitivity toward all the shades of grey, which can present sometimes as numbness and at other times as uncontrolled emotion. This numbness is also because contractions lack sensory context in the here and now: they are trapped energetic vibrations from the past. In this, their resonance can feel familiar, like a part of reality, or an old unliked family member. Consciousness effects contractions, awakening the condensed energy and bringing the permission of time and space that allows expansion. In this, the contracted energy is invited to return to source – rather like ice melting into water.

For a more comprehensive overview of Nondual Therapy, including a compendium of healing qualities and associated contractions, please refer to the earlier work: Nondual Therapy: The Psychology of Awakening [2].

In this book on passion, we focus on just one of the myriad qualities of consciousness. As you will discover, each quality is a doorway to the unbounded unity of true nature. Each is a perspective, or a way of perceiving. Each quality offers a portal to true nature, in which we access a timeless and limitless wealth of resources that empower our sacred passage of individual and collective evolution. This empowerment of the sacred rite of passage is called passion.

1. THE PASSION

Arousing the qualities of true nature

"You can't cross the sea merely by standing and staring at the water."

RABINDRANATH TAGORE

How would we begin to describe the nondual quality of passion? It is not a thing that can be held, possessed, or controlled, for passion can never be lost. It is neither active nor receptive nor still, but all of these, simultaneously. It is found in dazzling manifestations of form, and in the endless, impenetrable night, as the deeper, oblivious stirring of creative potential. It arises out of nothingness and with the manifesting charge of pure potential and freedom. It has intelligence beyond human design, and vitality of no man's making.

How would we show you passion? How would we arouse the sensuous unfolding of passion that longs to stir your unique version of life into being?

41

We cannot. We can only describe the edges and urge you to investigate, by saying again and again: "Look here, look here, look here." We can only signal the wordless expanse of passion by showing what it is not, where it has been fettered, where it is not yet free.

The journey is yours, and it is an honor to be part of it. This is an experiential journey, where finding our way depends on the felt sense. There is no map that can describe the multisensory unfolding of a nondual quality. There is no prior knowledge. It is a process of sentient revelation; a cracking, loosening, and liberating of energetic strata within all that we find ourselves to be. There is no map, and no prognosis for the living disclosure which is each individual life. This is part of the unfolding wonder of the sensuous, tactile, intelligent layers of being. This is the movement of passion.

Passion is found in the felt sense, but it is not the felt sense. In the same way that our seeing light is not the light itself, or the sense of movement is not the moving, we know passion by the felt sense, but it is not defined by our sense impressions. But sensory impressions of passion do offer footprints to follow into the source of the mystery. For passion is not an object, it is a living quality of consciousness. As conscious beings, we cannot control it, but we can blend with it. Where we perceive, we perceive through passion and what we perceive is passion manifesting. Where we receive, we receive through passion, and what we receive is passion returning. We are the passion, perceiving and receiving passion's many effects. Passion is the core movement of perceiving and receiving the whole.

For the author, as for the readers, this life is our passion. We are passionate about life, and we are passionate about true nature. Passion is so fundamental to the core of our manifestation, our vitality, our purpose, our love for one another, our wisdom and our destiny that this quality is one of the first to earn a volume of its own. It is a quality that dances with qualities such as love, care, belonging, need, fulfilment, freedom, manifestation, innocence, purity, esteem, salvation, direction, insight, genius, and unity. It can open the door to all true nature. It is in the impetus of arousal and the free-fall of release. Passion is a tremendous healer and changemaker. It moves with a sword of truth beyond polarities of right and wrong. It recruits all available vitality of any flavor. It is passion that brings the power of love, ferocious humility, righteous gratitude, and desperate care. Passion can transform fear to sensitivity, terror to exhilaration and horror to awe. It can move mountains and it will wait timelessly in the ripening of our becoming for the moment to arrive when it must flow.

Nondual Passion

Form does not differ from passion and passion does not differ from form. Form is passion and passion is form. Passion is the momentum within the bubbling of the unified field of intelligence spoken about by quantum cosmologist Prof. John Hagelin.[3] It is the vibration within the ocean of silence, the stirring within the sky of stillness, and the sub-unit within the field of emptiness. Within each atom, it is the quivering of the string, at the switch where fundamental particle is seen as pure energy. It is the preserving principle of every atom, that allows the containment of quantum power. It is the serving principle within the universe of every cell. At the essence of stillness, it empowers all movement bringing infinite possibility to each living moment. Passion is the energy through which the unmanifest manifests, transforms and releases back to source.

In this book, you will learn how passion is inseparable from compassion and how compassion is inseparable from wisdom. You will discover how life scientists are revealing the importance of passion even to our physical health. We will venture behind the tragicomic stage of judgmental mind and dualistic thinking, to find passion as that which demystifies moral norms to reveal deeper mystery.

Passion is beyond grasping and aversion and desire and denial. It is opened by our talents but arises from a deeper source than our individual gifts and skills. It is an open space of wonder and awe at the unknown. It is both perceptive and receptive, active, and unwinding. In the words of Albert Einstein: "I have no special talents. I am only passionately curious."

Exploring the deeper purpose of trauma, we will investigate how passion is at the tipping point between trauma and resilience, where suffering becomes both evolutionary and revolutionary. Where we are lost, passion brings direction. Where we despair, it allows insight, finding treasure in obscurity. Where we suffer, passion brings purpose. Where life lacks meaning, passion opens our senses within the lack, allowing a finer sensing of it all.

It could sound abstract and conceptual, but true passion is not a concept. It is not a question of will, but rather of surrender to the potency of our essential nature. We touch it by diving through our sensory aliveness, right into the existential continuum that is here, behind the in-breath and the out-breath. Take a few breaths in and out. Can you find it there, behind the inflow and outflow, and touch it?

Passion has been misconceived as uncontrolled sexuality or licentious behavior. It has been demonized as that forbidden freedom through which we destroy all well-behaved forms of life. But well-behaved is not the same as wellbeing. To find passion, we must be ready to unravel some of our mental conditioning and these dictates of behavior. Because passion has been condemned as dangerously close to freedom.

We hear of crimes of passion and understand that passion can be criminal. We know it has power, and we learn that uncontrolled power makes us bad. But passion is not antithetical to life, it is integral to all life. It is not the cause of sexual chaos but is the momentum within our deep and natural fertility. It is not criminal. But it has the power to dispel the very notion of badness, bringing compassion to the most neglected precincts of the human heart. It is not destructive, nor is it creative, but it will destroy and create whatever is needed according to a deeper intelligence of care. Passion is neither demonic nor angelic, it is the harmonizing force within it all. Passion is not that which brings suffering, it is the alchemy of transformation through which suffering becomes service to the whole.

Passion is at work in processes of learning, evolution, and survival. As the core momentum moving through the center of the body, it can shift us out of conceptual shafts of teacher and student, competition and collaboration, and success and failure. It spontaneously orients toward the wellbeing of the whole, delivering greater balance, harmony, direction, and fulfilment.

Passion is the magic which allows the opening of our senses, from crude sensation to more and more refined nuances of perception. When we are in passion, we move beyond the layers of fear, anger, and biological survival. We are ready to die in it, for it and in this, we move beyond the stranglehold of the fear of death. In this freedom and relaxation, we stop filtering our sense impressions. We move out of conflict. The mental censor resigns, as we are no longer compelled to keep a grip on reality. We move as a universal flow which is far more powerful than the instinct of separate preservation.

As the senses open, we enjoy increasing interchange with the environment. It feels as if we come to life. This too adds vitality and trains the nervous system in the instant reward of sensitivity. On a sensory level, passion moves us from fear of the unknown to the freedom of adventure.

Awakening the mind to the here and now, passion also brings the full power of eternity and infinity, the timeless and the boundless. We begin to master time, space, and measurement. Within time, this means we can have tremendous patience, or a pure sense of emergency. There is at once spontaneity and peace with time. With space, this means we expand endlessly, but also that we can move to zero distance, finding an easy unity with anything. There is freedom and intimacy in space. Because passion unlocks time and space, it unlocks freedom in form, which is movement.

With passion we can deeply relax in the wonder of paradox, being at once in the immediacy of bliss, and at the same time infinite and eternal. In this, passion reveals the deeper nature of consciousness itself.

When passion is denied it shows up in the contracted interplay of boredom and addiction. Boredom is the once-violent, now numb frustration of vitality. It resonates with senselessness and the lack of purpose. How does numbness feel to you? It is a kind of suffering, as if we traded our heroes for ghosts.

Addiction comes into play as an intense craving for what is compressed in that horribly boring numbness. We seek to release the repressed hunger, or the suppressed rage. We venture outside ourselves to find the passion we miss on the inside. Finding the suffering of boredom unbearably boring, we seek relief in the world, engaging the sense of reward through substance abuse or compulsive behaviors. We confuse temporary relief with fulfilment. This short-term effect and immediate gratification put pressure on the next dose of transient reward. A greater sense of inner lack comes forward, with tolerance for boredom even more reduced. We get caught in cycles of addiction that remove us from the center of our direct experience. Our consciousness gets scattered in alien notions of supply and demand, which are notions of limitation and lack. We find ourselves revenging the revenge and antidoting the antidotes. Seeking external tools to get control over suffering, we find ourselves possessed by it.

Passion is the conscious awakening of the vitality within experience, whether the experience is good or bad, comfortable, or atrocious. Most often, we deny our pain, so the vitality of passion forms a bottleneck in those areas. Yet suffering is evolutionary and is one with our sense of purpose. When suffering is denied, life begins to seem senseless. It loses meaning. We feel useless. We find ourselves feeling lost, in a soulless kind of futility, smothered beneath the added oppression of the energy of denial. All the time, the bottle neck of passion is building up, creating pressure. We long for unconditional release.

The darker side of our suffering – of the feelings we refuse to feel – is found in the active principle. We can find compassion for the wounded, abandoned, neglected parts of the psyche. But it can be much harder to find compassion for the voice of contempt, the wrong doer, the sadist, the betrayer, or the murderer. We are more likely to suffer hatred through feeling hated, for example, than by directly hating. We are caught in the belief in evil and the dread that we will be revealed as evil, deep down, so we deny it. We play victim to the endgame, when suddenly, unexpectedly, the form flips on its belly and we find ourselves writhing with aversion to life.

This is partly what gives passion a bad name. The energy released by the ultimate irrepressibility of passion can at first be suffering in the active form – the shamed, blamed, and horrified energy of the perpetrator. We see it where anxiety flips over out of sheer exhaustion and releases its voltage on the world in the form of rage. It is seen as madness and the failure to keep things together. It can have such a destructive charge that it can seem like the person "lost it." It can be reactive and harmful, but at a deeper layer it is a scream of pain or a wail of grief, a sound that has perhaps been muted by social force for generations. Also here, compassion must come.

Where our passion for life has been condemned, and out of confused loyalty we do not want to harm the environment, the voltage of passion turns back on itself. There is now a simmering rage of self-destruction. It is the suicidal zone, where the violence of kill or be killed retreats inside, in unthinkable prohibition. The pressure to release this contraction can display as acts of violence. When this violence is forbidden and judged, it too is forced back on itself and now the contraction is becoming a suicidal storm, which is also forbidden and judged. This is overlaid with an energy of badness and it too must be ignored and numbed. In this purposeless, murderous, senseless field of inner horror, we begin to feel sick indeed. Who would have thought that the simple, fresh passion for being alive in freedom could be the cause of such hellish pain? Who would look to this same passion as the remedy? Who would have thought that there are safe ways to channel the fire – such as the passion for peace, or the rage of mercy? Who would have thought that we could immediately, right now, in this moment, be free to be alive?

The psychological patterning of the nondual quality of passion through the energetic stuff of the separate self will be explored in this book. We hope with the words that follow, the passion in you is awakened in its unconditional purity and innocence, in such a way that it revitalizes the deeper sense of purpose and the freedom to move according to the compass of inner truth. To explore passion is to turn inside to a space of unconditional wholeness, and at the same time to turn outward, with a willingness to share the unique miracle of all that we are.

The invitation to passion is in you, with you and through you; right here and right now.

2. A SORRY STATE OF AFFAIRS

Taking leave of fake news

"If you're always trying to be normal, you will never know how amazing you can be."

MAYA ANGELOU

There's no point crying over spilled milk, yet the purpose and passion of these pages is to show you that there is. Our aim is to transmit something of the tremendous benefit available to all of us, when we manage to release some of the limitations we have around passion. Our refusal to cry over spilled milk is one of these. Our crying has no purpose, we are taught. It's redundant, because it can't un-spill the milk. It's senseless. Yet our crying has its own point, it is its own expression of loss, inseparable from all losses. The demand that we repress our pain is installed and updated by social norms. These unwritten codes of limitation and lack refute, pollute, and mute the naturalness of passion.

It all begins with debasing, vernacular catchphrases that coerce us as children into becoming small, inconsequential, and limited. It is a disowned semantic packaging passed from generation to generation, disguised as protective and yet crippling to the mind, heart and health. Like all conditioning, it talks through nonsensical idioms, consensual "realities", shadowy threats that we trusted – out of a longing to belong. We signed up to this system long before we could read the small print disclaimer disowning our brilliance. We got committed long before we knew that it would all end in tears.

"He thinks the sun shines out of his ass." This is a British expression which is at best humorous and at worst outright cruel. It's often used against someone who is passionate and alive with a mission. When he comes with a novel and brilliant idea, the admonishment can be: "Don't make waves," or "Don't rock the boat!" When he moves with esteem and without social fear, we will say he is "full of himself" and that he "thinks he owns the place." Pride comes before a fall as such people are condemned as "cocksure" or "big-headed" and "full of airs and graces." They are: "too big for their boots," and they think that: "the whole world revolves around them." Some might say that they constantly "blowing their own trumpet."

Even if they are inspired, idealistic, altruistic, and well-meaning, it will not help, as it's well known that: "The road to hell is paved with good intentions."

No wonder, when we, the accuser and the accused, feel a niggling itch of life, an impulse to create or find meaning, that we sabotage ourselves and feel ashamed of the secret wish to fulfil some deeper promise. It can only be selfish and narcissistic to want to be seen in the uniqueness of all we are. It's grandiose and attention seeking. Just the scent of it is asking for a good whipping, if not from the inner critic, then from the society of norms we all learned to hate and hate to love.

To use another tired idiom, the human psyche is indeed in: "A sorry state of affairs."

Yes, it is sorry – a word derived from the Old English sārig, meaning "pained, distressed", derived from West Germanic origin, from the base of the noun "sore". It is a kind of addiction to a state of suffering. We feel sore that we exist, sore that we make things hard on one another; sore that we're alive. This soreness is the apology we give for taking space and time, as if being here in time and space were an offence. We are sore in our movement, sore in our eminence, sore in our freedom, sore in our truth, and sore in our passion.

Within this sorry state of affairs, we look for permission from each other to be free, and we feel both dreadful and dreaded when we're not. Resentment grows, and our "sorry" becomes increasingly cynical. This sardonic disconnect, the suffering of which is also denied space, time, and permission, curdles into depression. Even the soreness gets sour. I'm so sorry that I'm sorry.

The depression, which was at first a feeling, in time becomes the lack of feeling, until at a certain stage there seems to be nothing there at all except a vaguely irritated boredom and perhaps some TV induced fantasy. From head to tail, from face to the place where the sun don't shine, we get numbed down, dumbed down, and messed around.

How would it be to really make waves, or to rock the boat without fear of capitulation, launching head-first into the river of life? How would it be to find ourselves free of the tyranny of the soreness of being, and to feel suddenly suffused with wondrous airs and graces? To notice that the sun shines brightly, unashamedly out of the ass; to know that you own this place; to be sure of your cock and to feel the bigness of your head, while standing in tight boots with the surefire knowledge that the whole universe is revolving around you, as you blow your own trumpet and pave a road to heaven or hell - or wherever is needed - with the pure gold of good intention?

How would it be to return to the playground of pure possibility, passionately alive and free?

To unlock and release the potential of the passion that can rise and move through all that we are, we need to reclaim the blueprint of the prison. Between states of boredom, resistance and depression, and the distractions of afflictive patterns, we need to find the cracking points. We need to let our pain be the fire of passion – moving from the helplessness, lack, and missing, to fury, vengeance, and the most outrageously embodied love for life.

For better or worse, through brimstone and fire, we need to get passionate about liberating the tidal power of passion. The truth of our pain feeds the fire of our passionate becoming.

There is no point crying over spilled milk, except for when there is.

Nondual Passion

3. ACCIDENTALLY ON PURPOSE

Awakening in the sense of purpose

"Ultimately, man should not ask what the meaning of his life is, but rather he must recognise that it is he who is asked."

VIKTOR FRANKL

If I were to ask you: What is your purpose in life? There is a chance you will begin thinking of an answer. Perhaps you will try to figure it out, this purpose, referring to outer authorities, or to the past. Sometimes, people look puzzled, suspecting an accusation of pointlessness, uselessness, or the horrific death-trap of failure. With confusion, fear arises, and a pressure to give an answer.

Knowing the answer calms the system, bringing stability, identity, and the confidence of being informed. But even when we come with an answer – my purpose is x or y – the answer itself can seem to expose a field of questions waiting to be born. There could be a background sense of the lie, a subtle frustration, a lingering expectation for a long-forgotten miracle, or an ancient sense of disappointment surfacing as fresh as the morning dew. How could we define our purpose? How could we limit it by making a "thing" of it? Somewhere, we shudder at the restriction.

Knowing our purpose is not always the same as finding it. Finding it means we have got a *sense* of it – in our heart, gut, and bones. Between finding our purpose, and knowing it, and living it, there can be whole rifts of despair. We can feel cheated by God, denied by the world, and betrayed by life. The pain of unfulfilled promise can be worse than no promise at all. We can feel a rageful disappointment or a dread of being that disappointment. So, sometimes it feels easier to shrug the promise of all we are born to be, because where there's such beauty we find only burden.

Burdened with the badness and sadness of it, disappointed and bored, we look for something to blame. The magical word "because" comes forward. Because puts a spell on us. When we say the word because, we empower something as being at cause of all that we are. When we say: "I can't be myself because of the system", for example, we give power to the system. We hypnotize ourselves into believing that the system is at cause of all we are. All we are is simply a helpless effect of the system. Each time we use the word because, we give away part of our vitality, part of our causality, part of our truth. We sacrifice our originality and our origination.

I am not free because of you. I can't find fulfilment because of my childhood. I am not happy because of the pain in my left foot. When we say because, we put our purpose in the field of illusion. We trade our true nature for an excuse. We try to shed the blame but find ourselves empowering the whole field of blame. I am not free because of the dog. Just imagine, the poor dog is now the cause, reason, meaning and definition of my freedom. We put the authority of our purpose outside of ourselves, surrounding ourselves with a social militia of should and should nots, and then we blame those same demigods that we feel so lost and so very alone.

> What does the sense of purpose feel like?

Our sense of purpose is intimately connected with the quality of passion. When we find a depth of purpose, we become alive and thrive. Purpose is the intelligence of passion. At the formational layer of the psyche, it activates the unique information within the individual. It brings our individuality to life. It offers the unique flavor of all we are into the collective field, making it useful, wherever it is needed. The joy in the fulfilment of the deeper need of the whole is inseparable from our intimate, individual sense of purpose.

In so many ways, to question our individual purpose is to question the purpose of life itself. This kind of question can be a catalyst of healing, an accelerator of transformation and a compass in our manifestation of true nature. Yet when we look for the sense of purpose, we will find it first and foremost as a sense. The answer will come from the felt sense – from the somatic sense of being alive. The sense of purpose is the sensing of purpose.

The purpose of life is found in the sense of purpose. It is in the feeling of mobilization in which individual skills and talents get orientated toward the wellbeing of the whole. There is a quickening of energetic flow, an arousal of the nerve system, a tingling charge of energy, and an alignment of head, heart, and body. This agreement between dimensions of experience lets us rest back as the source of all quality. Quality energy flows through us, merging with fields of resonance. The separate "I" becomes a perfunctory label, appearing here and there when its technically needed in service to the wider purpose and the deeper need.

Imagine a singer who is delivering a song to wore-torn soldiers. Traumatized and grief-struck, they are energetically melting into the tenderness of her voice, as her power and her melody supports them in the long journey back to the open heart. When her song is done, she steps off the stage.

"Hilda!" says a voice. "Hilda!!!" They need to call several times because she doesn't recognize her name. For a moment, the singer looks confused. Who the hell is Hilda?

Her whole being is still residing in the purpose of the song. Informed by the sense of purpose, the quality of passion had transported her beyond the limitations of the thinking mind and personal identity. As the song moves through her, so does the voice of heaven, calling its war-torn, forsaken children home.

The felt sense of purpose is primary, and the many ways it expresses through action are secondary. Purpose is not an idea, not a task, not a thought, but a feeling, a feeling that is intuitively arising out of the depth of need. The sense of purpose is the compass within passion. It gives direction to the manifestation of passion in life, and it consolidates us as an affirmative receiver of the expression of passion in others.

> "The more one forgets himself – by giving himself to a cause to serve or another person to love – the more human he is and the more he actualizes himself."
>
> Viktor Frankl

Yet we have a top-down approach to the world. We tend to believe that we are our thoughts and that our consciousness is also a kind of thought. This can give us a superficial feeling of control. At the same time, it generates a background atmosphere of victimhood and dreadful impotence. We are mentally required to manifest a purposeful reality, at the same time that we seem to constantly make a mess of it. This can leave us feeling lost, useless, and perpetually enslaved to the "other".

As slaves of thought, we actually contract our consciousness into a provisional control tower within the headquarters of the brain. From this contracted mental state, it can seem that the search and rescue of our purpose is a battle maneuver. Any success is in spite of the hostile environment of an unfriendly world. We are commanded to be purposeful, even while weathering the strange, unpredictable climate of our emotions and inner states. We must have purpose, even though we are attached to the strange enemy territory of a physical body. In a purposeless universe, gas-lighted by the gods, we are required to find purpose. We're born to bring heaven to earth, but God breaks the contract and makes it impossible for us. Devoid of the sense of purpose we can feel soulless and spiritually forsaken.

All this anguish is arising from a core conditioning that we are the thinking mind. Thinking defines us, or, "I think therefore I am." Yet so often, it is the thinking process that takes a simple sense of pain and whips up a whole psychic split. Our thoughts condemn us, criticize us, bully us, and abuse us. We complain at the world about our inner complaining and when this makes us feel awful, we despair a little more.

When we are split between thought and feeling, it can mean that on the one hand, we are raging against life, declaring it meaningless, while threatening god and wife with non-existence and personal suicide if we do not get what we desire; while on the other hand, we are stroking our dog with a tenderness that says we will never leave her. Do you recognize such splits in the psyche? Between the mental rage at senselessness, and the body's ongoing, natural, purposeful movements toward wellbeing?

When we look into nature, we will find an abundance of the sense of purpose. It seems that all forms of life are hardwired to experience it. When I give our dog a piece of sausage, she sometimes looks at it, like it is a senseless object. If I ask her to sit, lie down, follow me around the room and roll over, and then give her the same sausage, she is in ecstasies at its flavor. The sense of purpose draws out the deliciousness of life.

When you look to all animals, you can get a connection with the sense of purpose. It is in the way a bird flies with a twig in her mouth, in the awesome engineering of the bees in the hive, in the eminence of the trees, and in the industrious empires of a nest of ants. It is in the salmon, destined to swim upstream. It is in the cloud, decorating the sky as he waits for that moment where he must rain down.

The spiritual teacher Russel Williams[1] used to say that everything is perfect. It can be perfectly good, or perfectly bad. But it is perfect according to the conditions that surround it. It is the same with the sense of purpose.

Everything has its purpose, even the feeling of being useless has an undercurrent of the sense of purpose. Even our wildest declarations that life has no meaning, are broadcasting purpose through the frustration of purpose. Even absence, negation or non-being, have a sense of purpose. Why would this be? Could it be that the sense of purpose is integral to our consciousness? That wherever we are conscious and alive, we are blessed with the sense of purpose? Could it be that to follow the sense of purpose is to follow the light of consciousness? Could it be that this light of consciousness, or those spaces that light us up, are showing us the way we need to go to open our passion for life?

Nondual Passion

Georgi Y. Johnson

4. WHO DO YOU THINK YOU ARE?

Remembering the space beyond habitual thought

"When one is painting, one does not think."

RAPHAEL

What is a thought? Is it a sentence spoken by a voice inside the head? Such as: "Life is pointless"? So where are we in the space between thoughts? Who is there when the mind falls silent? What is the atmosphere of that silence? Could the differing flavors of silence be differing forms of thought? Could no thought be the opening to the greatest thoughts of all?

If we believe that the miracle of thought is the voice inside the separate head, then our beliefs have become senselessly narrow. Even when this voice offers knowledge, it is often orphaned from its environment, disconnected from its origin, and unable to penetrate the vital layers of experience.

Perhaps our thinking mind – the voice inside the head – can conjure up passion and purpose. There is a kind of sorcery possible, through the whipping up of emotional vibration through suggestion. However, it tends to conjure up emotion that is temporarily passionate, but then becomes just emotion. This is because the energy depletes without a central alignment to deeper subliminal yearnings and need. Its affect is shallow and short-term.

A voice inside the head without passion is like a word without a soul. Like in the words of Shakespeare's Hamlet: "My words fly up, my thoughts remain below. Words without thoughts never to heaven go." Such voices show what psychologists call "shallow affect" – which is a trait of psychopathy and other forms of mental disorder.

When we move out of the dictatorship of the voice inside the head, to the silent movie theatres of imagination, we find the same conditioned dislocation. That is, we are led to believe that our imagination somehow willfully dictates a reality, rather than being an expression of a deeper layer of feeling vibration.

If I were to ask you, right now, to imagine something - anything you like - what would it be?

Out of the field of infinite possibility, one image or fantasy appears. This, and no other. The image that appears is not random, although it is accidentally on purpose. It is an expression of a deeper vibration of feeling or emotion. It offers an image to represent a deeper area of experiential resonance. It is choice-less and informative, like so many conversations with life.

Can you sense the atmosphere of the thing that you just imagined?

Passion is not a thought. Thoughts can be passionate; they can be vehicles of passion, born of passion and transmitting passion. Yet thought is an expression of passion, just as an individual voice is the expression of a song.

Passion is not even a feeling or emotion (although these can also be passionate). Rather, feelings and emotions tend to be the effects of the movement of passion – just as the bending of the trees, or the rattling of shutters are the effects of a strong wind.

We consult our head to find our passion, to locate our purpose, and to search for meaning. Yet the head is destined to refer all questions to the felt sense of the present moment. Without feelings, thoughts are like corpses, they lack vitality and are missing a soul.

Thoughts are an expression of our being here, but they are not the origin of it. They can describe what is sensed, but when they dictate realities, they end up creating crusts of illusion over our living wholeness. Our thoughts – and language - can only describe what is happening at the basis of the body in the form of impressions. They can point toward the energization, the sense of power, the uprising of care, the liberation of truth that surround the movement of passion, but they cannot replace it.

Passion is a force stirring at the source of all physical manifestation. It is found as the dark, sentient wave before the arousal of physical sensation. It is one with the silence before the storm of thought. It is identical to the stillness within the turbulence of love. It is the forcefield of intelligence within the sacred compass of purpose found in each fundamental particle of matter.

Passion is not just a thought, like: "I'm passionate about passion." It is an impulse of all-powerful potential. Prior to any act, it is the power source of all activity. Prior to action, it arises spontaneously out of the living emptiness at the source of the actor. Unconditional to doing, it is often liberated through the undoing of our unique conditions of psychological slavery.

What energizes a thought, empowering it with the means to fly, is a resonance arising from beyond the structure of words. This resonance is alive as a sentient vibration, a vibration made possible by a force which is still more seminal.

As this uprising of passion happens within our individual circumference of experience, it takes every moment of history, every feature, tendency, pattern, strength, and weakness and puts it to work in service of the whole.

In this, the expression of passion is always awesomely unique, precious, and needed. As we begin to allow the movement of passion through all the forms of life around us, our chains snap and our being expands, made more vibrant with an existential light of unconditional freedom. All that we ever thought ourselves to be appears as irrelevant. All our fears fade to gray. Self-concern vanishes as we find ourselves in every self, as every self. Life is revealed in its preciousness as a physical moment of infinite opportunity.

We are not who we think we are.

Nondual Passion

5. IF YOU CAN'T MAKE IT, FAKE IT

When a quality complex is not quite the real deal

"A song is anything that can walk by itself."

BOB DYLAN

I f you can't make it, fake it. No, really, whole ideologies are promoting the fake orgasm of passion. There is a demand that we set goals for ourselves, take on projects, generate some ambition, and show signs of enthusiasm (even when it is not felt). In creating a sense of purpose, we are encouraged to use mental imagery, waste energies such as anger, greed or desire, and all kind of pornographic imaginations to get the system moving. It is part of that idolization of the thinking mind referred to in the last chapter.

The problem with this exaggerated investment in thought as defining reality is that it contracts the mind. Our thoughts become so preoccupied with thinking the right thing in order to get the right outcome that brings pleasure and not pain, that thinking itself becomes paralyzed. Our mental processers become so selective, that ignorance abounds.

This ignorance in time becomes forgetting. Where there were still shadows of experience, there are now blind spots. We literally become blind to uncomfortable thoughts and sensations – anything that could cause conflict or make us bad or sad.

These blind spots increase our feelings of insecurity in the environment. We feel unsafe, disconnected, alien. Most of the time, we don't know what's going on, and this not knowing is fearful, so we pretend to know stuff. We persuade ourselves that we're in control. But this pretense that aims to protect us, is itself under fire. Where we pretend, we could be exposed, so we have to be vigilant, careful of prying eyes. We get caught in a complex in which we desperately want to be seen, and yet really don't want to be seen in ways that we can't control. The whole interchange of conscious attention becomes risky.

As a coping strategy, to get some sense of safety back again, we work on our defenses and our pretenses. We cannot make it, so we fake it. But faking it makes us bad, it means we're not really seen, so it leaves us in our loneliness. We lose anyway.

Our neural networks become so conditioned in threat detection that many thoughts threaten thought itself: "It's crazy to think like that"; "I've got to get my head together"; "Amy is mad about Henry". Associations based on past trauma and suffering now become whole ideologies, fermented into structures of belief. Each belief is a voice spoken loudly in order to drown out the sound of its opposite. For example: "I'm in control of passion," is broadcast loudly and consciously enough to drown out its opposite: "passion will render us helpless."

It is immensely natural for us to be living expressions of passion. Passion is a healer, it gives direction, it is the living answer to the question intimately put to us by our incarnation. Passion is instantaneously fulfilling, and its movement brings unconditional reward. It is that which gives a sense that we are in the right place, at the right time, going in the right direction. It deliciously opens all the other nondual qualities. It contains the unique formula of our individual manifestation within unity. It brings health, vitality, but also deep rest and containment. It drastically diminishes the fear of death until all that is left is biological wonder.

Nondual Passion

Passion is not something we can win or lose. It is not something we can create or control. It is as autonomous as our life blood. Yet our conditioning has split our consciousness from this embodied passion.

We have the unblessed position of living through fragmentation, in which our thoughts compete in the head; our feelings compete in the ether; and our vitality competes with itself within the body. Our energetic constitution is locked in conflict, conspiracy, and contraction.

Although we might remember what it is to manifest passion, we suffer the disconnection from it. Just as we dismiss it, we miss it. Just as we scorn it, we mourn for it. Just as we feel deprived, we recall how passion helps us feel alive. We secretly crave passion, but recoil for how it could cause us to misbehave.

It seems impossible, or too dangerous, or too crazy, to just let this awesome, authentic force flow, uncensored. If we let your passion fly, we will surely "lose it". We split our life force to recklessness, lust, or craziness on the one hand, and rational, cool-headed, goal setting on the other. And of course, we must align with the latter if we want to survive. Grown-ups are rational and rationality is as cold as ice. Yet all of us are so longing for that deep glow of warmth which passion brings.

We want passion, but on our terms and conditions. This has a wash-out effect on the quantum power of the quality. Passion becomes ambition and ambition gets fixed on the next job, partner, status, or spiritual attainment. Just as the stuff that promises fulfillment is consumed, a hunger arises for more. The sense of inner lack or failure becomes incongruously sharper in direct proportion to our material gain. All the stuff in the world doesn't seem to be able to take this hunger away.

Passion bypass

In the realm of Nondual Therapy, this is where we find quality complexes. It's the principle of: "if you can't make it fake it." We solve the conundrum of uncontrolled true nature by recreating the quality at a safe distance from direct experience, so we can control it. In this way, we make a passion bypass. We use our will to skip over the vulnerability of core qualities by absorbing any shock or punishment or rejection into an artifice, rather than as a direct hit to the soul.

In our own ways, we develop quality complexes to try and extract reward without risk, pleasure without pain, freedom without loss, and delight without the shame. We try to get the benefit of the quality, while bypassing the pain.

A quality complex tries to tame the wildness of the soul. It shows up through structures of mental control. It takes unconditional aspects of source energy and tries to create safe conditions for manifestation.

We desperately miss the passion, which is part of our true nature, but we don't want the risk. We fear the shock and violation in our naturalness. We want passion, but we don't want to suffer. We know that this awesome quality is part of our uncooked potential, but these raw ingredients of life feel dangerous. They seem to threaten devastating consequences in the "real" world.

The problem is that we cannot live without our true nature. The qualities of our consciousness are ultimately irrepressible. So we strategize. We try to get the quality back on our own terms and under our own fear-based conditions. By faking a quality on the outside, incorporating it into the well-defended layer of ego, self-image, or controlled behavior, it feels safer. But it also degrades the soul.

We have learned that when we "appear" as compassionate, peaceful, or caring, we get positive feedback. Children learn that to pretend a quality – to do as if – can be an effective coping strategy. We defend ourselves with the appearance of qualities, in the hope that this will make us good, and prevent attack. We use the appearance of positive qualities as decoys to deflect animosity. For example, we smile happily when we are nervous; or when we are angry, we assume a serene face, because we have learned that our anger can trigger violence in others; or we pretend to be care about someone's misfortune, when secretly we couldn't give a damn.

When we suffer disconnection from a nondual quality, we begin to obsess about the areas where the sense of lack is strong. We demonstrate love; we declare freedom; we advocate innocence; and we protest that we care. We push ourselves ahead as passionate – promoting ourselves as focused, enthusiastic, and purposeful. We behave as if our work (that we really don't enjoy) really matters. Yet all the time, we generate an overdraft of shadow stuff. We feel prostituted through our inauthentic, pleasing behaviors, destructive like hell, and an inner cloud of rage builds up.

A quality complex is a beggar's portion of the feast of infinite abundance offered by our true nature. It is a remote, distressed echo of the core quality resonance. It is like the difference between a sugar lump in the mouth and the exquisite sweetness in the atmosphere around a new-born child. One is controlled, finite, addictive, easily lost and won through action; the other is unconditional, all-pervasive, truthful, and powerful beyond belief. One has a vulgarity that brings a whiplash in the world of effects, the other sustains us, arousing who we are at the essential layers of being. One enslaves us, the other reminds us that we are always, already free.

If there is such a difference between a quality complex and the real thing then why would we make the trade?

You could see a quality complex as being a movement of preservation. We dictate the qualities of true nature on life, as if they were not spontaneously part of life. After a while, we begin to believe that without our dictation, all will go to hell. The qualities are no longer seen as alive and given, but as the result of our mental effort and dictation. It's up to us to keep things good, but we get exhausted from the stress of it. All the passion of the universe we live in depends on our effort. It's a lot to ask.

Take heart

How can we tell if our passion is fake, for real, or a combination of fake and for real? You can sense it. Does it have a vibration of pretense? Is there a slight sense of forcing, or the stress of effort? If it's like this, it's OK. If you have a passion complex, it shows that the true passion is strong in you, or else you wouldn't miss it so much. The road inside is paved with gold. Be passionate about reclaiming space for the natural uprising of the true quality.

Our quality complexes have their downsides, but they also generate a field of possibility. We behave as if the passion is there, even when there's a psychological disconnect. The behavior does evoke a certain sentient attitude. For example, when we act "as if" we are loved, we might begin to experience ourselves as loveable, and unexpectedly, the inner environment might adjust to facilitate the direct experience of unconditional love. All nondual qualities are highly responsive to invitation.

So, when we deliberately speak with passion or purpose, act passionately, or instruct ourselves to feel passionate, the quality will arise. Yet it will then become limited by the conditions of the complex conditions that are born through the formulas of fear. A condition on passion could be that there will be no discomfort. When the condition is allowed to block the quality, we get a series of false starts. It makes for a bumpy ride. Still, it is a start.

When we do have a strong quality of passion, a passionless world where life has no purpose feels unbearable. So, we do something about it, we try to puff it up. We advertise that which we miss the most. We insist on the disconnected passion through our beliefs, moral codes, ethics, and standards of behavior. We demand attention, devotion, and selflessness. We forbid destruction, wild emotion, or spontaneity. We disagree with the world, god, and the universe over the existence of certain forms of cruelty and suffering. We forbid it. We develop a passion complex, which diagnostically shows us to return to the true nature of passion. Not the advertisement, not the agency, but the direct felt sense through body, heart, and mind.

The invitation here is to go for the quality of passion, with an open mind and with open senses, wherever is resonates, inside or outside ourselves, backward in time, or in the future. Be unconditional in the tuning into the passionate aspects of true nature. There is not a mite of dust without passion in it.

Unconditional means that yes, if needs be, let yourself fake it. Imagine what it would be like to feel passion, intimately, in the bones, muscle, and blood. Let passion be felt a zero distance. Notice the quality of passion in the vast spaces around you, even if it is means blending with the impersonal power or an ocean, or distant supernova

After faking it and making it, a third phase will emerge: maybe in a dream, perhaps in a moment of synchronicity. When the way is clear, passion will arise spontaneously, choicelessly, sneakily or wildly, out of the source within, or out of the universe as grace. Suddenly you will find passion directly expressing through all the forms of you, as the boundless quality of you, resonating as an inseparable and vital part of all you are.

And suddenly, with crisp clarity, it is no longer about you at all.

Nondual Passion

6. AN OPEN SECRET

Moving from possession to passion

"Lord free me of myself, so I can please you!"

MICHELANGELO

There is a lower magic about how we manifest realities. It teaches us that if we imagine we are already rich, already have that partner, or already have that job, then we will manifest that reality in physical life. "Your power is in your thoughts," writes Rhonda Byrne in the *The Secret*: "So stay awake. In other words, remember to remember." There's truth in it. Through generating a certain resonance within our thoughts in the present moment, we become co-creators of all future moments. We manifest our visions. Through the power of our minds, we can manifest reality.

It's all good, but when we look into it to the depth, the power is with the whole of mind, not just that conscious cusp where we think about what we want.

Nondual Passion

These principles of manifestation can sometimes actually widen the passion bypass by strengthening the personal agenda to avoid personal discomfort.

Often coming under the banner of the Law of Attraction, this popular ideology has left many frustrated, despairing individuals in its wake, swathed with the sense of failure that they have not managed to "manifest" the stuff they want in their lives. Rather than fulfilment, there is often an affirmation of failure. A deeper layer of thought rumbles from beneath the threshold of consciousness, such as the thought that there must be something wrong with me. The lack within the search for attainment gets stronger.

The notion of personal manifestation through strength of will and discipline of the mind is compelling and hypnotic, partly because it plays into the materialistic mainstream. The individual is demanded to get more, be more, do better and feel better. Rather than being celebrated in the unfolding mystery of our unique expression of humanity, we are measured, standardized and gift wrapped before we begin to breathe. Whatever it is about us that can be measured in time and space can never compare to the truth of our living individual brilliance. This unique light is irreplaceable, untradable and always ultimately undefinable. For example, can you really be defined by the car you drive? By the looks of your partner, or by the position you hold in a company?

Can such drops of limitation ever release the unlimited oceans of fulfilment for which we all long?

Hypnotic, repetitive advertisements of better versions of ourselves, ghosted with suggestions of current lack have groomed us in an addiction to self-deficiency disguised as self-sufficiency. Since the industrial revolution we have begun to equate our value with our wealth, our health with our stealth, and our success with what we possess.

We have been primed for lower magical thinking by our families, schools, religions, and nations. The good stuff, we are taught, is always on the outside. Without this inflow of good stuff, we lack goodness; we are not OK; we don't measure up; we lack value; and our birth has no worth. The race is on to make ourselves matter and for that we depend on the material world. The matter of the formless and wondrous aspects of experience such as the mystery of love doesn't matter too much. No surprise then, that so many of us find ourselves without passion, believing that to do what we love is to lack gravitas. What we love doesn't matter. Only real work matters, and real work takes effort.

We are under a spell of limitation. Driven forward by a stick bashing our ass with the threat of devaluation, disease, destitution, and death, we follow the carrot of material wealth. But the difference between us and those lovely donkeys is that they feel their pain, while we're sold stories and drugs to make it go away. Already as children, we learn to numb the distress of our slavery. All emotion is suspect. Too much excitement, enthusiasm and charge get us discharged from the class. We don't get graded on ease, but on effort and anything with value must take effort. But effort itself is based on the strain of never being good enough. In this, even our innermost passion is sacrificed in the temple of consumerism out of which the liturgy comes that we will never really succeed.

What we have not yet noticed is that if we were quintessentially made of success, then the only failure would be the failure to express the success that we anyway always are. When we are taught that we have to succeed on the outside, we are actually being taught that we are essentially a failure on the inside. We're taught that we are essentially enslaved and that the only way to get free, is through the power of our minds.

Somewhere in the past century there has been a switch from the idea of mind over matter as being slightly woo-woo and esoteric, to an endorsement of the notion that thoughts manifest our world. It has become the sociopolitical norm to believe that we can dictate reality. If the President says that the world pandemic is over, it's over, even when the virus thinks otherwise.

It's a dubious direction, because when we believe that the mind dictates reality, we come one step closer to mind control of the masses though the manipulation of big data and the mass media. This is because the separate self must always fail in dictating collective reality, as it is made of the same stuff as the collective reality. In the anguish of this failure, freedom gets lost as external temptations promise the "thing" that will bring success, or at least relief ; or the status that will make us safe, in which we'll be OK, and that will make the distress go away. When life continues with this distress anyway, all we can do is find ways to feel it less.

Rites of passage

When passion takes us over, then often the way we think can conflict with the pre-programmed, collective codes. There is a competition of realities or a war of the worlds. If the individual thoughts are too threatening, we can default to the binary principle that might is right. The individual reality is overpowered, judged, ridiculed, or incarcerated by the fear-based consensus. This consensus is found in the basic, dispassionate domain: that we must shutter down the suffering and get the pleasure while avoiding the pain. We lock down on life.

The idea of the lower magic is that because we are our thoughts, and our thoughts manifest reality, then we really must think the "right" things in order to be happy. We must control our thoughts, or else. While under this spell, we still believe that fulfillment is to be found through getting things from the outside. This kind of fulfilment depends on the notion that our wellbeing can be separated from the wellbeing of others, and the wellbeing of the whole. We are drugged into believing that our life must be earned, (that we have to earn a living), and that earning this life depends on winning against others. Life is not self-evident, it's a kind of weekend reward for our conforming to a state of conflict.

The law of attraction shows us that like attracts like, and that physical form will follow energetic resonance. But we get confused in the notion of control – that we can dictate our energy so as to dictate the resonance so as to get the dictated outcome. The very notion is seething with the atmosphere of neurosis, or the fear-based, stressed-out, moodiness of the control freak.

In the agenda to hack the age-old problem of suffering, the focus becomes selfish: it's all about personal relief and reward. Trading passion for ambition, we overlook those who have been hurt, forgotten, or exploited to achieve our personal success. We repress the deeper yearnings of the soul and the furious scream of the heart to be heard, seen and honored in those places where we have suffered the most. This is our deeper desire. It's in the hope of finally being honored in the truth of our lives. It is for this right to be seen, that all the wars of the worlds are waged. Yet our first premise is to get rid of the same pain that longs to be met.

Beliefs in personal manifestation based on material gain can isolate us. While gunning to become the winner and not the loser, to get success and not failure, pleasure and not pain, we can lose ourselves in caverns of inner isolation and despair. In our private happiness we are isolated and unsupported by the outer world. The fulfilling passages of deeper passion are blocked. Fulfillment, after all, is an energetic flow; it's a "filling up". If the channels of passion, love, peace, and freedom are blocked, how may we be fulfilled?

The isolation of the separate self through the drive to individually survive brings a viral load of limitations. In order to measure our success, we must objectify as a finite "thing". Finite things die. They can be damaged, violated, rejected, and enslaved. In trying to be bigger, better and more, we find ourselves suddenly small: closed minded, tight fisted, mean hearted and somehow still jealous of the ungraspable contentment that others seem to possess. Are they cheating?

The scope of sensitivity and responsiveness gets reduced to the shady borders of me, myself, and I. Our hard-won manifestation can seem to be not a bang, but a whimper.

Nondual Passion

The popular culture of personal manifestation has enticed a generation into an ideology of personal gain that generates a sense of separation from the whole. The disconnect from the field of unity evokes an inner loss of epic proportions. This can feel unbearable, so we numb it down, boarding up the inner world still more as a no-go zone. The question of the state of the union must be met on the outside, by being better, smarter, or trying harder.

The blocked passages inside the psyche are suffused with the inner sense of boredom, blankness, or nothingness. The lack of safe passage to the inner world means we take a conscious bypass into the outer world. The outer world makes sense, the inner world feels senseless. You would not expect it, but boredom and the dense sense of nothingness are a tremendous suffering. It's like having a numb pelvis, or not feeling the weight in a leg. It's bewildering, frustrating and it gets us out of balance. When we lose balance, we grasp at something to hold onto in the world of objects. We are again clinging to the outer world., losing our center as we become seekers on a quest to do something, get something or score something to fill up the void. But whatever we get, it is never good enough.

The lower magic of mind control delivers a superficial crust of experience that barely conceals the bodily dread of pain that haunts the diaphragm and disrupts our breath. This is because when we willfully focus our thoughts on a reality that we want we're always also focusing on the cause of our wanting – which is that which we don't want. We broadcast the lack behind that thought.

Based on resonance, the law of attraction says that like attracts like. Happy thoughts attract happy things. But this has a depth. Happy thoughts on existential despair will attract existential despair and a happy thought. Thoughts of attainment born of unsafety, attract unsafety and a whole load of stuff. Thoughts of nondual liberation based on aversion to a dualistic world will birth dualism and aversion, with a nondual face. Sooner or later, our living energy will catch us off guard, when our personal agendas have been put to sleep for the night.

There is a vast difference between looking happy and being happy. The field of resonance is way deeper than the tip of the iceberg which is our conscious mind. For example, when we are bringing the bank balance of $30 million into the present moment, we are also bringing the method beneath that wish – the dread of poverty, the existential fear, the slavery to money, and on and on. We are consciously affirming and recreating a whole reality – which contains that same energetic suffering that caused us to want $30 million in the first place. Only now we have $30 million more in the bank to lose.

Lack on lack

When we fantasize about what we want, as if we already have it in real time, in order to manifest it later, we are also investing in fantasy. Each moment of illusion births another moment of illusion. Each fantasy vibration births the next la-la vibration. Even that physical Mercedes Benz will have a slightly fake, illusory quality to it. Make-believe breeds make-believe. Intoxication demands toxicity.

The sense of lack is a form of suffering just like any other. It might pretend to be non-existent, but that non-existence has a flavor, albeit an uncomfortable one. The sense of lack resonates in the area of poverty, neglect, starvation, thirst, isolation and unmet need. When we invest our consciousness in the sense of lack, we make it stronger

Whatever the desire, it is driven by a sense of lack, and when lack is the power beneath the wanting, the future results of the mental hocus pocus will be equally alive with lack. We lose our natural direction, as the sense of lack takes over. $30 million cannot buy an exemption. No amount of money and no quantity of cosmetic surgery can buy us out of this sense of lack. Pure lack is not even a bad thing, but it's our aversion to it that makes it bad.

It is not a crime to want stuff and to seek status. We all do it, as we are coded by this software of seeking. But the realization that this illusion is just causing more suffering is part of our evolution.

When we turn back inside, we find that our suffering does matter. It matters to us. Out of the awakening of the truth within our suffering, passion emerges, which branches into compassion and flowers as wisdom. The evolution is of body, heart and mind and the quality of passion is the primary agent of growth.

We became so addicted to dictating experience, that we are losing our receptivity – our ability to sense and feel the spontaneity of living impressions in the here and now. Not knowing exactly what is going on around us makes us unsafe and generates an amorphous sense of threat. This sense of threat directs us to avoid the unknown still more, as the unknown could hide horrible outcomes (such as disease, incarceration, death). In this way, we lose our way. We get numb to the sense of purpose and our passion often goes offline.

What is it that we truly desire? Can we sense what is really needed, in this moment, for our personal manifestation? If fulfillment is our destiny, do we remember what fulfillment feels like?

In our boredom on the inside and addiction to the outside, we have by degrees forgotten how to feel. The senses get dulled, and the thoughts get increasingly dumbed down. We no longer wait for the earth to speak to us, or the cells of the body to reveal their genius, so we stop listening, stop asking, and block the energy exchange. After a while, we stop believing in any revelation, and because we stop believing, we stop experiencing. We become cynical indeed, but cynical in a bored, negative, contemptuous way - not yet cynical enough to take a sword of truth and slash down the veils of illusion.

In this, our individual purpose has become scripted as a future based agenda, rather than as the felt sense of purpose that lives as a compass in this here and now. Our passion has been traded for fashion and the ambition to get somewhere else, be someone else, and to feel something else.

Could we dare to be magnificent?

Could it be that wherever we see magnificence that this magnificence is alive in us? Could it be that whatever we dream up as fulfilment from our position as a fearful work-in-process could never compare to what the universe has planned for us? That to follow the plan, we first need to open up the body, heart, and mind to the authenticity of all that we feel?

Could it be that the deeper secret and the higher magic is right in the heart of those areas where we suffer the most, in those same areas that we have always avoided?

There is an offering of passion beyond belief waiting at the door of every individual, but it is a door which is often closed. It is the door through which we perceive and receive life unfiltered and without control. Are we ready to let it open?

This offering of passion leaves no part untended. It touches the form, but also the soul of the form. It arouses suffering but also the creational power within the pain. It welcomes adversity but also the hero within the moment of strife. It takes the horror of death and instantly holds the wonder of life.

It will not forsake the forsaken nor expel the refugee. It will not despise the despicable, nor will it reject that which has been hounded out of form. Rather it will turn to each thread of physical, energetic, sentient, and spiritual vibration as if it were meeting the miracle. This is the alchemy in which suffering becomes passion, passion becomes purpose, and purpose becomes manifestation. All this is suffused with the sense of unconditional reward and fulfillment - a reunion of life with life.

This is the deeper secret and the higher magic. Our sense of purpose and our passion is right here, in the cracking open of the intimate kernel of our suffering, in an offering of service to the whole. In this, we stop creating illusion and open to the sense of truth, sharing it all in the light of conscious arousal.

7. THROUGH HELL AND HIGH WATER

How suffering is the power source of passion

"My Lord, why hast thou forsaken me?"

JESUS CHRIST

So far, we have established that we are often distracted from passion by social pressure. We have shown how passion has become confused with mental agenda and the thinking mind; how we are indoctrinated into the "top-down" approach in which our brain is supposed to give direction, meaning and purpose to experience. We also ventured into the whole area of quality complexes, where we pretend to be passionate in order to get a sense of passion, which often shows how much we miss and long for that spontaneous, choiceless fire of who we are at the experiential core.

Nondual Passion

In the previous chapter we looked at how the New Age fashion of manifesting our reality often falls short of fulfillment, forsaking both the reason and season of our brilliance in its need for immediate gratification. It misses the depth, truth, and wholeness of experience, due to its agenda to selectively keep the stuff that feels "good" and get rid of the stuff that feels "bad".

Now, stepping beneath the divisive mechanics of the judgmental mind, we are going to explore passion. But to do this, we need to look deeply into the nature of experience, and especially into the nature of the vibration of experience we call suffering.

In the 13th century, the word suffering emerged, with the meaning: "allow to occur or continue, permit, tolerate, fail to prevent or suppress..." By the late 14th century, it already took on the meaning: "to undergo, be subject to, be affected by, experience; be acted on by an agent." In short, the word suffering, in its origin, is synonymous with the word experience, especially the helplessness within experience.

Suffering in its purest sense is found here, right at the psychic junction between suffering and resistance (resistance, which as an experience can also be a form of suffering). In its original sense, to suffer something is to allow it. So, when we agree to suffer our own being here, there is a "yes" to life. Where there is resistance, or resistance toward the resistance, we are saying "no" to life, and forming conditions on our aliveness. Yet we are that life, before we say either yes or no to it. The life we suffer, or resist is the same life that suffers and resists. The splitting of life from life is another form of experience within the whole.

Both suffering and resistance are reflexes within the purity of helplessness. This helplessness is at the core of all experience. It is the pure openness that allows passion to emerge. The admission of helplessness can be the golden key to opening the mind, heart, and body. Helplessness brings the softening into the imperceivable power source of pure potential that allows the awakening of the passion for life.

When we resist something which is anyway happening, then we become victimized. The thing we resist gets externalized and we lose agency, suffering in a more dissipated form. The original resonance of suffering is still there, but we splinter it with the additional resonance of resistance. We do this by deflecting our consciousness, and then wonder why we feel deflected.

Our ability to suffer directly relates to our ability to experience anything at all. The less we are able to contain uncomfortable impressions and sensations, the more we shut down on experience in general.

Nondual Passion

The more we are able to suffer our lives, the greater is our empowerment and agency. The very agreement to suffer arises out of a depth of internal authority that precedes experience of any kind. By agreeing to allow the pain within experience, we affirm that we are at source not caught in the experience; we are not possessed by it nor are we defined by it. Experience is perpetually changing, but we remain. We are the perceptive space that watches and feels the ebb and flow of all impressions. This affirmation of our inner authority and spaciousness further increases our ability to freely allow experience. We relax still deeper into the permission to be physically alive, and then as we relax, the senses open. Colors become brighter, sounds become clearer, and we begin to taste, smell, and touch the world in fresh ways. As we move out of the fog of denial, we begin to come to life.

We are conditioned into a belief that our resistance proves our strength. We confuse resistance with resilience. But on examination, we can find that when we resist an aspect of experience, we lose power. Resilience is about adaptability, flexibility, and responsiveness to change. It's not the rigidification of resistance.

When we believe that we need to resist something, we are investing in the belief in weakness. Something in us could be broken, so resistance is necessary. In this we give our power to that which we are resisting. What we resist, persists. We are no longer the subject which is the experiencer. Rather, we identify as the passive object that is being acted upon. We turn on our heels and go on the run, sometimes for so long that we forget what we are running from. This disempowerment, disenfranchisement, discrimination, disappointment, disgrace, distress, or distraction (just choose your "dis" word), further limits our ability to come to life.

To suffer, or to resist? Either way, there is a real psychological sense of destiny delayed. At worst, our resistance can obscure our consciousness so effectively that we lose connection with the very wellbeing we have been striving for, forgetting even that such wellbeing exists. It is a dualistic predicament described succinctly by Shakespeare's Hamlet in the timeless soliloquy on the paradox of being alive:

> *"To be, or not to be, that is the question: Whether 'tis nobler in the mind to suffer the slings and arrows of outrageous fortune, or to take arms against a sea of troubles, and by opposing end them: to die, to sleep, no more; and by a sleep, to say we end the heartache, and the thousand natural shocks that flesh is heir to? 'Tis a consummation devoutly to be wished. To die to sleep, to sleep, perchance to dream; Aye, there's the rub, for in that sleep of death what dreams may come when we have shuffled off this mortal coil, must give us pause."*

Prolonged resistance is only possible through a reduction in sensitivity – a form of psychic sleep. Within this sleep, the same denied suffering emerges in dream-like form, still seeking release, only now it lacks physical context and appears as the ravings of a disturbed mind.

As long as all is pleasure, comfort and joy, experience is sweetly welcomed, we would think. Yet what happens over time is that when we repeatedly deny the sense of suffering, we begin to distrust all experience. Because experience is full of unwanted surprises and the only way we can control it is to deny its spontaneity and rehearse it, censor it, filter it, and dull the lights on it.

It's simply not possible to take the suffering out of experience, but still, from season to season, without sense or reason, we try. The sense of love is tagged with future loss, so we lose the loving. We shun the sense of peace because we already know we'll be shocked by conflict. We reject our innocence because our badness is a foregone conclusion. We shun our purity because who would want pure filth?

The very nature of conscious awakening is that it appears through differentiation – often through the abrasive effect of something new or "other than I". That is, all experience is to some degree uncomfortable. If there were no dissonance between our deeper self and our experience, would there be any experience at all?

If we were made of the color blue, and the exact same color blue were to appear before us, would we even be able to sense it? How could we sense the temperature of the air if that temperature were precisely the same as our bodily heat? Experience is generated through the sensual stress of difference, through the vulnerability within variety, and through the shock of conflict. It all disturbs the peace. It rocks the stillness of the water. It is the light that arouses the spirits of the night and it casts shadows, everywhere. From one perspective, all experience is a kind of suffering. If we wish to experience life, we must be ready to suffer it. It is out of this readiness to come to life, that passion arises.

All our darkest nightmares and our wildest dreams are formed out of areas of conflict seeking resolution. These apparitions are externalized, appearing outwardly as "other" than us. Suffering is "ex"-perience, and experience is a core effect of creation. Creation is a manifestation of trial and error, driven by need, and in this, we are co-creators. As we experience, we experiment, and as we experiment, we learn, which is our evolution. We are hard-wired for this adventure.

That means that the whole world - whether it is our oyster or not - is made of the suffering that we spend much of our lives trying to avoid, at the same time that we try to ensure that it lasts forever, because endings hurt, loss is dreadful, and death is the ending we learned to believe in. Yet in this great evolutionary playing field, governed by multiplication and division, we have this free choice between suffering and resistance.

Resistance is all about buying more time and space, in order to preserve form so that experience can evolve. It gives us the means to temporarily slow the rate of change, and to process experience in digestible chunks. Yet when this natural resistance gets hijacked by fear which in turn finds danger in all forms of experience, whether deemed good or bad, we get into trouble. We lose our balance.

Every moment of creation is also a moment of destruction. When we create something new, we destroy the old. When we create an adult, we destroy the child. When we create a painting, we destroy the whiteness of the canvass. When we build a house, we tear into the earth, uproot trees, and disrupt the flight paths of birds. When we create a new human form, we also create a new human death. Endings are implicit to beginnings, just as every arrival already contains departure. The attempt to take the suffering out of life is like trying

Passion

(n.) c. 1200, from Late Latin Passionem (nominative passio) "suffering, enduring," from past-participle stem of Latin pati "to endure, undergo, experience..."

to take the wetness out of water. The only way we can avoid the wetness of water is by numbing the senses altogether.

When our purpose is hijacked by an agenda to get only the comfort and not the discomfort, we become uncomfortably numb. This shows up as states of existential boredom and pointlessness (see Chapter 12). Resistance stiffens the limbs and slows the vitality in the body in a kind of existential passive aggression towards the experience of being alive.

The agenda to take the suffering out of experience breeds an exponential field of conflict and confusion around the original suffering. This is because impermanence is a key ingredient to every moment – including moments of bliss, beauty, ecstasy, and joy. And this impermanence brings loss, sadness, and grief. This is why the Buddhists refer to the suffering of impermanence – which is also, thankfully, the impermanence of suffering. Where we resist, we also resist the mercy of impermanence.

Nondual Passion

If we could take the grief out of our experience, we would also be paralyzing the timeless joy found in that which was lost. If we could remove the loss from our lives, we would also remove the gain. We would remove movement itself. If we could prevent the pain of parting, we would also prevent the passion of penetration. All depends on the underlying wholeness of experiential awareness in order to thrive. In the words of Khalil Gibran:

> *"Your joy is your sorrow unmasked.*
>
> *And the selfsame well from which your laughter rises was oftentimes filled with your tears.*
>
> *And how else can it be?*
>
> *The deeper that sorrow carves into your being, the more joy you can contain."*

If we try to take the suffering out of experience, we lose some of our capacity to experience anything at all. The formula of grief is found in the joy shared with the one that was lost. The key information in the pain of rejection is found in the sense of belonging. The very internal structure of boredom is the passion which has been frustrated.

And this is where it gets interesting. The word "suffering" is synonymous with the word "passion". Passion is the raw flame of experience; the essence of suffering; the consciousness at the core of all manifestation. To pass is to step through, to move, or to permit. If to suffer is to allow experience to live in us, then passion is to permit the broadcast of that experience.

We can recall that the passage of suffering, crucifixion, and resurrection is traditionally called the Passion of Christ. In this circulation from heaven, to earth, to hell and to heaven, we are shown a natural circulation of form and transformation that is indigenous to the very nature of experience.

In suffering, we suffer our aliveness – we allow the varieties of experience to flavor our consciousness. In passion, we offer our inner world through a transformative process back to the whole - to be shared, expressed, and broadcast as part of our unified evolutionary purpose.

When we get hurt, there is vitality in it. The first cuts are the deepest. They are meaningful because they have a sense of truth about them. When we are hurt to the core, we feel our core. This centers us and brings a sense of purpose. When something cuts us to the quick, there is a quickening of vibration. We awaken to what is essential. This includes the timeless, existential core of ourselves found within our true nature. The deeper the wounding, the more \startling the opportunity for conscious awakening. Suffering is a catalyst for conscious awakening. It is a rude awakening, but it is an awakening of magnificent, healing proportions.

8. SAVING GRACES

The alchemical power of passion

*"For things to reveal themselves to us, we need to be
ready to abandon our views about them."*

THICH NHAT HANH

Suffering has vitality in it. It is charged with frustrated quality energy. Our deeper suffering defines us. Moments of affliction where we were cut to the core reverberate at the shores of deeper feeling, referencing every awakened moment. Where suffering is denied, these moments form floors to the psyche, layers of habitual stress between us and the imagined horror beneath. Our past suffering has an ongoing, formative effect on the way we experience life. It informs our decisions and directs our consciousness. It tells us when to stay and when to run. When we awaken in the night, these moments of suffering are with us. They are loyal passengers on the journey of life.

Nondual Passion

The moments where we have suffered are flames lighting up the timeline of our personal history. They show where we have been ignited, where something in us burned, is burning and will continue to burn. This is the light of our aliveness. It offers purpose, insight, and direction. It can become a kind of secret resource – if we let it. When we follow the path within, illuminated by the torches of old pain, it can lead us back to the original fire of passion.

When we remove our judgement about suffering and agree to suffer the suffering without grasping or aversion, a journey begins which is energized by the sense of truth. It is a journey made in the here and now, and to take it, sometimes all that is needed is to show up for the next step.

This attendance to the pain that has formed us means that we step over the barbed wire of judgmental mind. We sober up from the self-destructive tendency to heap guilt and accusation on our suffering, declaring it as "bad". This dumping of badness on old pain is like physically assaulting those wounded by an accident. It takes a temporal challenge met on the bumpy road of life and turns it into a timeless atrocity. This self judgement in the places where we suffer has become a way to deny the pain, as denial makes it hurt less in the short term. It brings some placebo relief, but it can't negate what has happened, the impact of which runs far deeper than our conscious awareness.

Where we judge our pain, we overlay our pain with the energy of judgment. Can you tune into the atmosphere of the judgmental mind? Is it friendly? Could it offer healing? Our faculty of judgment is here to work for us, not against us. Rather than heaping badness, and shame on the spaces where we suffer, it could be operating as an advocate of time and space, structuring the supply of whatever is needed to process the pain.

Judgmentalism is the signature of the fractured psyche. We judge where we are divided inside. We spit judgments out of the psychic split. There is a war going on inside. We make our sense of badness bad, and close down our feeling abilities. We shame our sense of shame, as if the sense of shame were disgusting. We forsake our sadness, as if our tears would never stop. We hate our hatred, despise our jealousy, revile our revulsion, and fail to visit our loneliness. In our judgmental tendencies, we lose compassion, and where we lose compassion, we become unwise and apathetic. This sentient apathy starts to seek out pain as a way to feel alive. Most often it seeks out the pain of the other, even to inflict pain on others.

To move beyond this tendency to desensitize ourselves to our intimate suffering, we need to change our attitude toward the ways in which we suffer. The insight that suffering is the raw material of passion and the whole blessed purpose of our lives can help with this.

There is a kind of alchemy that happens when we agree to suffer our lives. At first, it might seem depressing, unbearable, or overwhelming. This sense of overwhelm is also a sensation, not a fact. The feeling of overwhelm is a suffering. When we give time, space, and permission to the sense of overwhelm, what happens?

We can take all the time and all the space that we need. We have infinity and eternity at our command. Knowing that we are masters of time and space within our inner world supports our ability to let sensations of overwhelm be alive. And when we can allow the sensations, we find that we are suddenly more spacious than we ever imagined. We are not the overwhelming content, but the spacious awareness that allows it to live.

Amazing grace

Let us take a moment to venture into this space out of which we allow the experience of suffering. To get to that pivotal place of permission, we need to draw inward to a space that is even deeper than the agony. We need to get behind the agony if we are going to allow it. It is a deeper passion that gives us that power to step deeper even than our most intense private pain. We step over the inner cliff-edge of our misery and find that we are falling into the mystery. We are falling and rising through the thresholds of the unknown, our spirit infiltrating the essential, pluripotent passageways of all experience. Passion re-centers our consciousness at the source of itself. The temporal spell of pain is punctured as we fall into wider spaces of grace. The grace of our true nature releases and it now pervades all the places of pain with the permission to be alive.

As we begin daring direct experience, we get strengthened in the consciousness that is able to allow experience. When we learn how to die within our pain, we find that we are deathless. We might even become curious about what other precious fragments of our past are waiting to be unearthed.

At a certain stage, the art of suffering becomes fluid. We no longer identify too much with the content of experience, but rather willingly enter fields of suffering, knowing that they are the sentient landscape of all of us. In this, the sense of suffering might vastly increase, yet at the same time, we are able to contain it without stress. The sense of suffering increases, but at the same time decreases, as it is no longer personal, and we are no longer alone but belonging together. We become calm in the art of living.

Now, we can even visit dimensions of abandonment, or hells of despair. Where we are aware, we care, and in undercutting the trance of suffering we have found that we are boundlessly aware, so we boundlessly care. Supported by the wisdom of impermanence, we agree to enter the meadows of isolation, and the valleys of the shadow of death. We know that there is hard, painful, sentient territory, but we also know that even with all the shadows of doubt, we will pass through. Because the territory of experience does not define us. We are unrestrained. We can open our arms to the disfigurement of jealousy, meet the cold gaze of absence, and find vocation in the forsaken.

In this unholy exposure to the vast suffering within the whole creative endeavor, a holy rage ignites. This existential fire rises as passion, fueled by a determination to let it go, let it be and let it be for real. As passion flares up, it is fired not by self-concern but by truth. A transformative light breaks the bardo land of forgotten fragments of life. This light exposes fields of need. Empowered and empowering, it awakens a divine, sacredly human sense of purpose. Let's try to make it better.

As passion arises, every fiber of form is aroused. There is a quickening of the whole energy system. The nerve system is no longer surviving but thriving. Charged with the vitality of quality energy we offer ourselves to the inner fire of transformation. It can feel as if rivers could burst their banks, or as if we are smoldering through the surface of our skin. There is a sense of bliss, a sense of endless power. We're ready to sweep aside any obstruction to the passage of this passionate awakening.

Our vulnerability to fear and threat wilts, as with each place where we move through passion, there is immediate fulfillment and reward. This immediacy brings us into the present moment and energizes us still more, as the whole entity starts moving with purpose and direction.

Passion is not a concept; it is an energetic uprising. It is not something that we think or dream up, it is something that is felt. If we do have thoughts and dreams, they are sourced in these primary undercurrents of passion. These passionate undercurrents of the psyche give subliminal direction to our lives.

Passion does not flow out of the head and into the body, but rather surges upward out of the depths of our physical presence. It passes the beacon of light through our guts, through our blood, to our hearts. It is also part of the ancestral legacy, timelessly waiting in the bones and in every cell of the body for the activation of the pluripotent stem cells of infinite possibility.

How will we find passion? By following the trail of the felt sense, moment by moment, in the here and now. By taking up the sense of truth and journeying into the inner world, through the needle's eye of the shocking fact of our own existence. By picking up the path lit by moments of past pain and trusting it. By letting passion burn bright, wherever she might appear. By doing what we love and by loving what we do. By being for real, moment by moment, bravely stepping into the unpredictable yet profoundly easy truth of the here and the now.

9. ALCHEMY OF TRUE NATURE

From suffering, to absence, to passion, to purpose

"He is metallic yet liquid, matter yet spirit, cold yet fiery, poison and yet healing draught – a symbol uniting all the opposites."

C.G. JUNG, PSYCHOLOGY AND ALCHEMY

OK, so the suggestion of a personal crucifixion is probably not that appealing. You might have begun this book looking to get rid of suffering, not to get more of it. But we are in it for the long game, which is not just the passing moments of pleasure, but the eternal moments of well-being. We are not here to surf a little wave of purpose, but to realize the majesty and unspeakable fulfilment of becoming the ocean. And along the way, in meeting the long-sectioned parts of the psyche we have learned to avoid, we will also uncover some of the living formulas of heroism and healing.

Every compact parcel of pain contains within it an exponential healing gin. First, it contains within it the healing of itself. There is no such thing as an unhealable energetic wound. In the same proportion as the pain of the wounding, so must the blissful release of healing appear, for the energies of wounding and healing depend on one another. Just as the experience contracts, so must it release. Second, the wounding contains the healing formula for all pain, of any nature. Third, the wounding opens and heals the past, and the future. Fourth, it heals all around itself, through a contagious resonance of transformative healing energy. Last but not least, it offers the beauty and power of resilience through fundamental shifts in attitude to life itself. From one point of view, where we are wounded, we are also blessed. There are blessings embedded in our woundedness.

What is another difference between passion and suffering? The word suffering is used for all those impressions that we have judged as bad. The word passion is used for all those expressions we deem as dangerous.

When we judge an experience as bad, we change our perception of it: our consciousness adopts an attitude of badness. This could show up as shame, hatred, revulsion, scorn, or contempt. The resonance of this badness mixes into the felt sense, making the experience even worse.

For judgement, we need two parts. It's connected with the pain of division or split. In nonduality, the suffering of the pain of separation is primary. The pain of separation persuades us that we are ultimately alone. That sense of badness is a big part of that pain. It is found in the suffering of the separate self, the energetic stuff at the border between ourselves and others where we have been shocked or violated in our naturalness. While suffering is the impression of this pain of separation. Passion is the healing of it.

Most of the time, the shock of separation happens when we are rejected. For example, perhaps there was an atmosphere of contempt between our parents. We stand between them, and unwittingly become the target of wrath. The suffering of the separate self is not the kind of pain that comes with vitality and truth, most often it is a second-hand, inherited, senseless kind of suffering, in which we lose power, motivation, and purpose. The world appears as senseless, strange, passionless, and deranged.

Our response to the bewildering pain of separation is often to thicken the energetic substance of the separate self. Promising psychological immunity, the separate self actually increases the sense of badness and sadness, by adding to it the fears of violation and isolation.

The world is split haphazardly into inner and outer, and we have to constantly arbitrate what is what. Just because our sensitivity has decreased, it doesn't mean we have gained wellbeing. Rather, we begin to define ourselves according to this baseline of disease. Separation defines us, and we are commanded to be better and more than others, or else we find ourselves feeling worse and less. It's an unfriendly struggle of preparing for tomorrow, comparing yesterdays and repairing the damage from an unfriendly world. We complain at what we disdain and disdain what makes us complain. All change is fearful as change brings the stranger and the stranger is a danger. But estranged from deeper need and disengaged from truth, the real danger is often the stranger we suddenly find ourselves to be.

The idea of the "separate self" promises immunity, but there is no separate self, and the promise of immunity has left us confused. Seeking relief through disconnection, we are left with the horror of disconnection within an ongoing, irrefutable connection. The relief we really needed was for more time and space for our inner world, for greater warmth, affirmation, and permission to be free. We needed to find true release as the unconditional field behind all differentiation, rather than to be objectified, oppressed, repressed, and depressed within condensed energies of aversion.

Judgment makes us bad, and that badness makes us sad. The badness and the sadness we fear and refuse to feel becomes condensed as judgmental waste matter at the energetic borders of the separate self. It divides us between inside and outside, self, and other, and enslaves us to fear. We become afraid to manifest and terrified of accidentally expressing our naturalness. It gets hard to relax, even in the company of the ones that would naturally be supporting us. In this, fear is the cruel taskmaster. When it makes us run, jump, and hide, we are in the grip of fear. Following the formulas of fear, we lose our way. We even become confused in the biological pathways of pure, natural, responsive, and healthy fear. We are so busy with the fears around the separate self that we often become insensitive to actual approaching danger. Our instinctive, attuned, biological fear gets hijacked by an astral fear, that threatens formlessly and never gets resolved. Passion has the sharpness to cut through the illusion of fear and awaken us to the endless scope of feeling sensitivity contracted within it. Passion offers the alchemy that will transmute fear to love.

Sometimes, in order to find that unconditional release into the inner universe we need to let ourselves be conquered. To find passion, we need to be brave in our vulnerability and pain. Only then do we see that the invading army could actually be our allies.

It can feel like we are going insane, as if we are disintegrating in pain, no longer holding it together, getting devoured by a predator. We have no option but to be helpless in this pain. In this, we truly allow the pain, and we merge with it, becoming it. There are no longer two competing fields of experience. Instead, there is one whole which begins to expand. We become whole as the suffering and the suffering becomes part of our wholeness. We become more purely alive. Something in the energetic armor of the separate self is vanquished.

Out of this emptiness, released from the purgatory of judgmental mind, out of the bottomless relief of choiceless helplessness, life begins to stir as an existential power. We find we are still here, existing as the unified field of infinite possibility, deathless, alive. Suffering again begins to awaken, but now it rises as passion with all the resources of true nature.

Passion is the alchemy in the transmutation from fear to love. It is that which can bust the boundary of fear, threat and pain between inner and outer worlds and blow up the illusions of dread. It has that momentum and that unifying power.

Although it might unearth the suffering foundations of the separate self, passion is not dangerous. It will not make us unsafe. On the contrary, it empowers us. It brings an evolved, conversant, alive form of immunity, an immunity won through understanding, information exchange and connection. Passion is like a long-lost, loving, laughing, warm, protecting father has finally returned to the heart of the family, and to every wounded child he touches along the way he gives the kiss of life.

Nondual Passion

10. PASSPORT TO EVERYWHERE

Passing through the substance of the separate self

"Passion is energy. Feel the power that comes from focusing on what excites you."

OPRAH WINFREY

Passion is a passage of source vitality through the energetic boundaries of the separate self. It passes through the makeshift border between self and "other". These borders are made of the denser energy of suffering. They block the flow of refined energy through their energetic density, mass, and weight. The energy that congeals as the border of the separate self is heavy, depressed, contracted and compressed. It is made of our disinherited despair, our numbed anger, and our tranquillized fear. This "stuff" of separation comes forward in the division between ourselves and others, or between the inner world and the outer.

The splitting of experience into outer and inner worlds has many frontiers. There is a split between us and the universe; between ourselves and nature; between ourselves and God; between ourselves and our fellow human. There are even internal splits between us and ourselves – between who we are and who we want to be, or between our thoughts, feelings, and physical experience. When we talk about holistic medicine, or transpersonal healing, we are generally thinking beyond that split. Yet for many forms of therapy, the fractured psyche is the alpha and omega of the therapeutic approach. It is an assumed reality.

The energetic stuff that divides the psyche between inner and outer worlds – the substance of the separate self – is dense. It is energy in contraction. For example, if love were water in flow, then the contracted form of it would show up as hatred or the energy of self-sacrifice. It is brittle, and so cold that it burns. This hatred is shocked love. It is made of love. In the same way, the energy of boredom is sedated passion.

Contracted energy which is at the border of the separate self is made up of all the varieties of suffering where we have been shocked or wounded in our naturalness. It includes the energy of resistance, the numbed pain of rejection, and the dumbed down sense of stupidity.

These sufferings of disconnection are real, even though they resonate within the fact of connection. The pain of separation happens within the fact of wholeness. We believe it is an actual disconnection, but it is rather the change in flavor of connection from nurture to torture. The bewildered mind translates the suffering of the separate self as a fixed fact, so that it can regain control. But this is just a belief, it is no longer true to the ebb and flow of experience.

The suffering of the sense of separation does not mean we are actually separated. In the same manner, the suffering of resistance to life does not mean that we have the power to resist life. Life cannot resist life. It can only create divisions and splits within mental consciousness. Life goes on, undisturbed.

The energetic stuff of the separate self is often also weighted with the sense of guilt or wrongness. All this is often sealed with the acid of shame.

This energetic glue of the separate self presumes authority over who, what and where we are. It seems to define us. Defined by the pain of separation, we forget who we really are – which is the undefinable source of all life and all form. It is so much easier for the mind to identify with something, than a formless nothing. When we objectify ourselves, it can be easier to believe that we're in control. We've got a grip on ourselves. But out of this objectification, fear is born.

We start to compare the object of ourselves to other people, whom we also objectify. We start to compete. We weave whole illusory stories, often dictating who and what other people are in order to compare them to who or what we are. Yet we do not really know who anyone is at all. Whole sentient craters of suffering are opened in the psyche, where we suffer the dread of condemnation, abandonment, and loneliness.

We need other people as fundamentally as we need oxygen to be alive. Through the inflow and outflow of energy, we become affirmed in our individuality. It is togetherness that makes us unique, not the opposite. The free flow of energy through the suffering stuff of the separate self is profoundly supportive of wellbeing. We need one another, our wellbeing demands it. No form of life can survive for long in disconnection from its living environment. Through each other, we expand, grow, heal, and evolve. Through each other, we are able to remember who we are. In the words of the pioneering expert on trauma Dr. Bessel van der Kolk:

> *"Social support is not the same as merely being in the presence of others. The critical issue is reciprocity: being truly heard and seen by the people around us, feeling that we are held in someone else's*

mind and heart. For our physiology to calm down, heal, and grow we need a visceral feeling of safety. No doctor can write a prescription for friendship and love." [9]

The notion of the separate self is a pandemic of suffering and stress. The stuff of separation, being energetically dense, can begin to feel more "real" than our consciousness. This is because each time we forget about it and look again, it is still there. It's a stubborn energy created and confirmed by all that we've learned. This includes the devolved norms of our education systems and the barrage of mass media messages that reinforce the experience that the "real world" is a world of objects.

Objectification – taking a series of impressions from the felt sense and making an objective "thing" of it – has become an addiction and a compulsion. We take the objects we created in the past and we hurl them at one another, defining our future based on past conclusions. All this enforces the increasingly familiar, uncomfortably numb stress of isolation that creates tension between ourselves and the environment.

Dancing to the consensual melody of this software of suffering, the energetic stuff of the separate self, blocks the flow of sentient information in all directions - from outside-in, and from inside-out. It becomes hard for us to let the world in, and harder for us to freely express ourselves.

Nondual Passion

What is the effect on the substance of the separate self when passion begins to pass over its muddy slopes?

When passion stirs through the psyche there is a clearance, and a fresh sense of space and awake-ness. This allows us to come into an alignment of head, heart, and body. It is not that suddenly life is all pleasure. If it all, it becomes more serious than ever before, and yet much less entangled. There is power in the movement of passion, which means there is far less chance of becoming distracted by minor discomforts. It is as if the soul undergoes a reorientation within the body. We find our ground, we rise, and we stand tall, irrespective of social fear.

By degrees, we become less reactive to small matters as every fiber of experience becomes devoted to the same movement of passion. This brings the sense of purpose, direction, and reward. As the perimeters of the separate self becomes less obsessive, an inner stillness becomes accessible. As body, heart and mind become responsive to the needs in the here and now, the energetic substance of the separate self itself begins to change constitution. Where it was never actually there in the first place, it is no longer mentally imagined. Where there are contractions from histories of pain and trauma, there is a melting. The felt sense of resistance, depression, and numbness mutates into a freshness and an easy emotional intensity. The whole form is coming to life, moving, and transforming through the deeper power of passion.

It can feel like we have been dragging through our days in an awkward and heavy suit of armor. The wardrobes of war are now getting exchanged into whole new wardrobes of endless possibility. Our appearance to the outside is no longer a front-line coping strategy. What we wear, the outer skin of the separate self, is no longer sought as the source of fulfilment, protection, and self-expression. It is no longer our compass through which we find direction. How we appear to others no longer has authority over how we are. We have switched gear into the quality streams of passion.

However, this protective armor of the separate self was worn for a reason. In a way, it is the accumulation of generations of defensive measures against being shocked, wounded, or violated. We don't need to let it all go at once. We can always put it on again if there's danger. But as the armor begins to have chinks in it, and the passion flows through, we find we need it less and less. At first, we might feel an ecstasy of manifestation, but soon afterward an incredible vulnerability. There is a healing whiplash to the break-down of the separate self, and this whiplash, handled with tenderness and permission, is also healing.

Passion whiplash

Part of the passion whiplash can be sourced in generational trauma. These emotions need our care and patience. These repressed areas of experience have waited generations to be felt, to scream, speak, rage and to spit hatred. When we can give some space and time to what has passed through the history of our physiology, they will find their correct and honored place in the truth of their own context. (We will go more into passion and ancestry in Chapter 21).

Another part of the whiplash of our disintegrating shell can be connected to the actual lack of safety in our environment, pointing to a need to find skillful means to let passion move without too much danger. Often that safer environment is available to us. We just forgot that we have the right to it. If your immediate environment sucks, passion will show you where you have the freedom to change it.

As passion moves, our sensitivity and emotion begin to work for us, rather than against us. This has the healing effect of changing our attitude towards our emotions, and towards life.

There can be a flash of anger, for example. This anger is brighter, less sticky, and more responsive to real-time need. There is less badness in it. It is corrective and then easily released. Often, it will work for the purpose within

> What would we need to be able to relax?

the passion – setting boundaries, clearing the way of obstacles, accelerating movement. It releases emotional vitality for the service of the greater good. This is where we might find holy rage, furious humility, or a rant of wisdom. It is a far cry from the spooky rage that brews backstage when the movement of passion has been frustrated.

In a similar purification, our fear turns through the alchemy of passion into sensitivity. Our psychic antenna become alive as receivers of information. There is a greater sensory refinement. Colors are seen as brighter; sounds are clearer and more varied; atmospheres near and far become more accessible to sampling. Each thread of experience quivers in the here and now.

The fearful arousal of the nerve system that was previously shunned now affirms the safety of being informed in real-time by the resonant environment. This connectivity brings a deeper relaxation and this relaxation means we can connect more deeply to others, free of the sense of burden, guilt, or obligation. In relaxation, we open, and this opening further widens the passage for passion.

Yet there is a reason why we are in a habitual state of stress. There were reasons why we did not relax until now. We could not relax, because then we would feel something unpleasant or uncomfortable. Now, these underlying vulnerabilities are being kissed by the energy of passion.

Arising directly out of the source of all we are, passion is full of healing potential. It has the power to draw the core qualities out of the energetic contraction of the separate self.

Where there is self-hatred, the possibility of love will emerge. Where there is slavery, there will be the scent of freedom. Where there is shame, it will shine so purely it shatters the heart. Where there is guilt, green shoots of innocence will break through the miasma. Humility will show her limitless strength at the core of jealousy. Indisputable belonging will rage out of the subterfuge of conditional acceptance. Absence and abandonment will tremble with a lullaby of care. And as joy appears as a great, existential sun behind the weathering of grief, eternity stands endlessly upright at the centrifuge of time.

The end of suffering

Passion is the end of suffering, but it is not the cessation of it.

When we are moved by passion, or when we become passion on the move, then what was previously seen as an endless ocean of suffering can now be seen as having a beginning, a middle and an end.

Our difficulty in allowing experience is connected to our difficulties with the structure of time. When passion awakens, it reveals that suffering is passing with time. What had appeared as eternal pain is now seen as pain changing through the eyes of eternity. Our pain comes and goes, and we remain, as the continuum beneath the pulse of experience. The suffering of transience becomes the transience of suffering.

When we become passion on the move, then what was previously felt as an infinity of pain, as a bottomless pit of suffering, can now be sensed as only occupying a certain area, and as a limited portion of space. There is a place where suffering ends, and fresh air begins. There can even be an ocean of suffering, but above it, the stillness of a clear sky. There is a shape to suffering. There is an inside and outside, a before and behind, an above and below.

Our difficulty in allowing experience is connected to our difficulty with the structure of space. This shows up as difficulty containing any emotion or feeling. When we unlock the passion for life, it becomes clear that our suffering takes up a restricted amount of space and that even this is unstable. It is changing shape, in a constant process of transformation. This whole process of living transformation is occurring within the boundless field of our undifferentiated awareness. Suffering is changing, we are not. The suffering of impermanence becomes the impermanence of suffering.

When passion awakens, or when we awaken as passion, it liberates the infinite possibility of feeling and sense perception. Arising out of the unified field of infinite potential, passion brings passage through all that is limited in time and space. Arising as the formless, we are empowered as the source beneath all form. Alive as the formless source of all experience, we emerge as masters of form.

When we shift into the inner authority of our passion, we learn new ways to navigate the river of life. Whereas previously, we complained about the unpredictability of the river, trying to dictate its course to decrease our pain, now we are learning how to sail with its mysterious journey. Passion is a sacred passage - all the way to the ocean.

11. COMPASSION IS ALL ABOUT YOU

From passion, to compassion, to wisdom, and back

"My mission in life is not merely to survive, but to thrive; and to do so with some passion, some compassion, some humor, and some style."

MAYA ANGELOU

There is an endless source of evolutionary power available to us, commanding us to live, to manifest, and to express our true nature into the world.

When we follow our passion, the movement brings an immediate sense of reward and the unconditional sense of purpose, direction, and fulfilment. It is as if something clicks into place in the here and now. The compass within passion is the sense of purpose. This sense of purpose seeks out the real-time need, guided by the wisdom of the greatest good for the greatest number. It seeks to contribute, to be useful. The sense of purpose brings a quickening of energy, recruiting and releasing vitality for manifestation. Through the sense of purpose, we see that the nondual quality of passion, from the core, seeks to be of service to the whole. There is an integral devotion to wellbeing, an inherent dedication to life, and a congenital care for creation.

Where we surrender into the internal uprising of passion, the whole universe seems to meet us. There is an alignment between individual need and the need of the whole. The passion that is intimately inside us is showing up as universal passion. With harmonic resonance, like attracts like. Quality energy attracts quality energy. This law of attraction is called compassion.

Out of the unified source of life, one passion emerges. As it enters physical vibration, it differentiates into varied expressions. Yet it is one source expressing through the manifold, rather like one light shining through windowpanes of different colors. When the passion in us recognizes the same passion in the "other", it's called compassion.

Remember that passion as a word is synonymous with suffering which is synonymous with experience. Compassion is the direct wisdom that we are one in passion, suffering and all experience. It is the heart-felt and natural manifestation of the wisdom of unity and the wisdom of interdependence. Indeed, this circulation of passion, compassion, and wisdom through dimensions of body, heart and mind is fundamental to manifestation. It is an all-powerful, transformative trilogy that can shatter and recreate the sense of self.

Compassion is at the core of the law of attraction – the resonant principle of like attracting like. That is why, when we move from passion, or from the truth of our own experience, it can seem that the universe aligns with us. The universe is compassionate. But it is also why we are often attracted to others in whom there is a vibration of suffering that has been denied within ourselves. In a way, we fall in love with the suffering we sense in others, often because we are unable to love it in ourselves.

Compassion is a core healing principle within the physical dimension. It is the transformative, evolutionary drive toward well-being that means we find purpose through one another. This is precisely due to the temporary differentiation into separate form. Yet, when I am of service to you, you are of service to me, and we are of service to the liberation of the whole.

Suffering is part of all experience within creation. At certain frequencies, love is a suffering. It mashes up who we think we are, disrupts our habitual states, and breaks us up until we seem to disappear.

The same could be said of all nondual qualities. Innocence can register as agony. Just think of the look in the eyes of a tortured animal. Purity can burn us. Freedom can manifest as terrifying destruction. Even space can show up as the most unbearable absence. This is the intimate and sublime, beautiful and disastrous, horrific, and awesome, cruel, and tender, blissful, and torturous playing field of created form.

The law of compassion affirms that we are in it together. We depend on one another. Your wellbeing is my wellbeing. The health of the planet is our health. The happiness of animals is our happiness. The bliss of exploding stars is universal bliss. We are not only inseparable within the unified source of all, we are also inseparable within the fields of experience. We move with every vibration of life, as we are ourselves responsive, connected, interdependent vibrations of life. We are always affected by each other.

The unified source of pure potential to which we have been referring is at the eye of conscious awareness. It is at the open source of pure singularity and has been referred to as the eye that cannot see itself. It is the central doorway of our perception. Out of this field, passion arises and manifests through the world of form. It feels like an expansion or an active movement. Yet, as has been made clear, it is simultaneously a movement of allowance or receptivity. There is a pulling power in the presence behind our senses that invites impressions. Indeed, all our senses are fundamentally receptive.

As we begin to manifest through layers of form, there is an event horizon in which we succumb to the pulling power at the point of singularity in another person. We are drawn into their point of view. We are moved to see things from their perspective, as if we were in their shoes. We experience through the form of the "other". There is a deep passion at play in this movement of compassion. As with all the nondual qualities, it has a creative principle, which is the reunion of source with itself, through evolving vibrations of form.

What creates space for this movement is the pure emptiness of all experience – of all those impressions which are dancing with time and changing through space. The emptiness is that alchemical gap where suffering becomes passion; and it is there in the shock of difference through which passion becomes compassion. It is the primal rift that is part of all creation and all creative processes – the point of perceptive singularity behind all experience.

Nondual Passion

The whole universe is hardwired for compassion. Even at the level of fundamental particles (the smallest building blocks of matter), we find the principle of quantum entanglement. Called by Einstein "spooky action at a distance", entangled particles remain connected and effected by one another even when separated by vast distances. A change in one causes a change in the other. One way to explain this could be through the timeless, zero-distance unity found at the point of singularity within each particle. This point of singularity is with you, in you right now, watching behind the one that is watching.

Our brains are also hardwired for compassion. Mirror neurons, sometimes called "empathy neurons" respond to a witnessed experience in another as if it were happening to us. That is, we watch someone eating and we begin to salivate. We see someone bashed on the hand, and we compassionately grab out own hand. Before the pre-frontal cortex intervenes with the executive decision that this is "not me", we experience all impressions personally. Even after we have made that differentiation, it is possible to have open-ended empathy through the firing of mirror neurons. We do not need to actively walk a mile in the moccasins of another, we are already doing it. Even if our processing of the information is overlaid with the thick energy of resistance.

On a cellular level, our bodies are in a constant compassionate exchange with the environment through each in-breath and out-breath. To say it with broad brushstrokes, we are breathing in questions and breathing out answers, sometimes in the form of evolved questions. This interdependency of all forms of life only appears cursed when it is perceived through the lens of personal self-interest or arrogance. There is a vast biological information exchange happening that is orientated toward the wellbeing of the whole.

Within each body, there is also intracellular compassion. The purpose of each cell is not to separately survive but to support the wellbeing and health of the whole. A cell will even take on its specific task according to the pull of need within the whole. For example, there will be a flood of neuronal stem cells when there is a need to accelerate learning through the processing of new forms of experience.

Compassion is ubiquitous and natural, yet in our quest for individual distinction, we learned to ignore this sentient, living law that governs all forms of experience. We forgot its benefits.

It's all about you

It is one of the socio-cultural ironies of our generation that in our striving for individual achievement, we lost compassion for ourselves as individuals.

Seeking social acceptance, we stifle our emotions, hating our own aversion and getting inwardly furious when we feel anger. Looking for beauty in the eyes of an imagined audience, we let our bodies be sliced and our flesh be amputated by the surgeon's knife. We shame our loneliness and punish ourselves for feeling wrong. We revile our perceived imperfections, and we starve ourselves where we miss nurture. Even qualities such as compassion and care can be used to bypass the pain within the individual psyche – as we seek personal relief by trying to "fix" pain in the safer territory of the psyche of the "other".

In general compassion is about surrendering to the pull of need, not about fixing, changing, or getting rid of pain. The core need within all pain is for it to become conscious. Consciousness within pain allows the revelation of the remedy. The revelation of the remedy is often already the remedy. For example, when the pain of rejection becomes conscious, the need for a sense of belonging is revealed. The sense of belonging has already become resonantly alive within the pain of rejection. When our consciousness bypasses pain by trying to get rid of it before it is experienced, the remedy for the pain is also bypassed.

Self-compassion is not about creating an objective self. Quite the opposite. It is about letting what we thought was an objective self, melt back as a field of living impressions. Then, the experience of being alive, including the experience of pain, is liberated within the pure field of our awareness. When we do not condemn pain or go to the war with pain, awareness itself offers the natural invitation toward healing and reunion with the whole.

When the quality of passion is released, a powerful self-compassion emerges. This is because we move out of the paradigm of "good-ism". Beyond the judgement of good or bad, passion moves with truth. Truthfulness – the authenticity of experience – overrides the agenda to be good, to be loving or to be caring in order to not be rejected. In this, it brings permission and validation to many parts of the psyche that have been disowned – such as those areas where we feel unlovable, despicable, or worthless. When passion is on the move, these parts also belong. Because the movement is no longer about the acceptability of the little "me", movement becomes free. We are now moved by an existential need which is far greater than any defensive idea of "self".

The destiny of passion is compassion of heart and wisdom of mind. Compassion opens communication, companionship, community, and communion. It is the comfort we find in commonality, and the living, interconnected expression of passion for the purpose of the whole. The core of suffering is passion. It is in the sublime, creative rupture that is there when one universe breaks apart to release another. It is arched with unspeakable aloneness and sorrow; and yet, as with every birth process, it is the passage to new life.

At the core of the sense of purpose within the quality of passion is an unconditional, non-negotiable care for all living forms. Even in not caring, we care. We care because we are there. We care because we share. Our prayer is our care, and we care, choicelessly, wherever we are aware.

12. WHEN NOTHING MATTERS

Boredom is not nothing, it is sedated passion

"I would rather die of passion than of boredom."

ÉMILE ZOLA

Passion is a primal nondual quality inseparable from the "big bang", or the creative impetus of the whole physical universe. This explosive force is inseparable from the birth of consciousness and mind, which includes the splitting between subject and object, perceiver and perceived. It is a cosmic, experiential event taking place within the indivisible space of pure awareness.

This boundless, perceptive infinity of our pure awareness – the backdrop to consciousness, creation, and movement – is so all-prevalent and omnipresent that we began to ignore it. We learned to relate to our ubiquitous presence behind all experience as "nothing". Because it is not a "thing" in a perceived universe of interacting things, we devalued it. Only things have value; only things matter; only things can make an impact. Nothing is impotent, ineffective, and irrelevant. Nothing has no purpose, and because it is useless, it is also senseless. Nothing means nothing to us. Nothing appears to be the absence of anything. Yet nothing is the source of everything. Out of nothing, all passion emerges.

Yes, in this chapter, we are going to make much ado about nothing.

Like a prodigal child that wonders into the wilderness, our consciousness loses itself and longs to return. Seeking the fulfilment of home, it searches for things to shake off that lonely sense of lostness. It searches for something to make it feel whole – the missing "thing". Yet the last place we search is deep within the thickets of ignorance, in the unpromising, thing-less, dispassionate emptiness of "nothing".

When we ignore the infinite sky of our pure awareness, we fill the space with the energy of ignorance. This ignorance has a density of denial, resistance, and refusal. This density splits our perception, obscuring our view, and giving the appearance of division. The life inside at first seems to be separated from the life outside. Outside appears as active, inside as passive. Outside grabs our attention, inside gets ignored. Soon, it can seem there is no life inside at all – just a wall of nothing. this nothing is now experienced as a dead zone – a no-go area where nothing can be gained as nothing moves and nothing lives. We begin to believe that there is nothing there. We recoil from the density of it. It seems to repulse us.

Why would we ignore the infinity of our awareness?

Ignorance is born as a reflexive response to suffering. The creation of the physical universe is painful. It involves rupture, rapture, expansion, and contraction. Out of our free will, we can delay the experience of the pain, by retracting our consciousness from the experience. When we pull consciousness away, there is a collapse. The area of pain shrinks, but it also gets a greater density – rather like a balloon with the air released. This density is made of contracted passion – the blissful, explosive, existential power of creative manifestation.

The retraction of consciousness and the contraction into density desensitizes the passion. What had been overwhelmingly painful is now comfortably numb. What had been expanding into infinity is now reduced to the dimensions of a "thing" – a thing we call "nothing". We keep our "nothing" in bite-sized, tasteless portions, forming a barrier between our concept of self, and the limitless source of all that we are. The experience we meet when we touch this energy is that there is nothing moving. It is tremendously boring.

The fear-based impulse to contract (deny, repress, compress, suppress) our passion enforces the fear-based belief that passion cannot be trusted. In this way, fear gets empowered and begins to manipulate our sense of purpose and to control our direction.

Through contracting our passion, the fear of losing mental control is contained, at the same time as the illusion of mind control is enforced. Also, here, the mind contracts, as it begins to act as if it cannot be trusted.

A belief forms that our thoughts needs to be controlled, in order that we may stay in control. This feeds a belief that if we (the mind) lose control (of the mind) we will go insane. We desperately try to "keep our head together", without knowing where to go to get instructions. The imperative is to be controlled. As we are mentally the problem, we begin to seek out authorities outside of ourselves. We refer ourselves and our sense of reality to an external, objective reality of "things", or to a consensual belief system. Energetically, we sell ourselves to the loudest bidder.

In a wilderness of "things", life becomes increasingly senseless. A background energy of boredom taunts us from the inside, like a passive-aggressive family member, full of undefined accusations. But this so-called boredom is made of passion waiting to explode into life. It is a kingdom of compressed, infinite potential. All we need is the courage to really give it space so we can experience it. It is a blessed passage of consciousness to a reunion with passion.

Passion is a quality that is full of infinite possibility. In its active principle it is charged with undifferentiated vitality. It speaks before it thinks, screams to be heard, shreds consensual denial, and cuts through delusion with a sword of direction. Before the censoring mind has an inkling of what is coming, passion stirs up the biochemistry of the body and lights up the central nervous system. Its fast energy seeks equally fast release through expression and manifestation. With energy for the short or the long haul, its uncompromising staying power brings austerity, authenticity, and authority. This is the quality that can move mountains or that can navigate the eye of a needle. It is a force to be reckoned with.

To counter this force – to be able to turn it into something as insentient as boredom – we need to hijack a lot of vitality. This vitality is taken from the passion itself. We turn the energy of passion against passion with an agenda to keep it quiet. This frustrated passion begins to vibrate with what we would now call rage. Rage is passion which has been judged – passion which has been infused with the energy of badness. The threat that passion poses to the status quo is turned against itself. It now feels both rageful and threatened – a silent fury. Can you sense how this energy shakes within the body when it is denied its natural flow?

But now, if we were to express the passion, it could well show up as violence. It is perfumed with badness and ill intent from prior condemnation. As a boundless threat of evil, it seals its own fate. It gets judged and denied again. More badness is injected into it. The condensed malevolence within the rigidified energy of boredom is now becoming quite sinister. Who would want to taste it?

This badness is so horrible to feel, that our consciousness retracts still further, creating an even denser strata of ignorance. Ignorance is insensitive, lacking curiosity and profoundly boring. This energy of boredom is so unbearable that we could become violent to try and break out of it. If we get sucked into the field of boredom, it can feel like being buried alive. Literally – it can feel like our intimate soul and all its blessed vitality is buried within a totally unfitting density.

To add more woe to injury, we are tormented by seemingly lifeless habits and patterns, mini, self-serving addictive cycles aimed to release the pressure, that are innately lifeless and incapacitated in terms of bringing any real satisfaction.

The boredom becomes apocryphal. The earth of the body quakes around its unholy insentience.

As parts of the naturally fluid psyche move into rigor mortis, other parts start to panic. We begin to psychologically react through patterns of stress and depression. The whole psycho-physical ecology gets out of balance. All because of the simple matter of nothing.

Healing is a *U-turn* of consciousness. Instead of moving away from the field of affliction – the area of boredom or numbness – consciousness moves with care and curiosity toward it. The invitation of consciousness is to allow what is contracted to expand, revealing the sentient ingredients of the frozen energy.

There can be a sense of irritation, an atmosphere of badness, or a seething resentment at being unfairly accused showing up with the poisonous scent of injustice. There can be shame and the agony of rejection. We can even touch the ubiquitous human suffering of suicidal despair, where a forbidden violence is turning in on itself in a hellish, perpetual threat of an endgame. It is not accidental that our unleashed passion has sometimes been associated with the realms of hell.

Just as passion arises out of the field of infinite source potential, passion in contraction has the potential for every flavor of suffering. Each recipe of pain will be uniquely formulated according to its psychological etiology. But now, rather than being judged, rejected, or scorned, this frozen energy is invited to dance within the conscious experience. When conscious awareness opens the felt sense, there is infinite space and endless time available for what was contracted to expand and to take on a life of its own with a voice of its own. This voice has often been waiting for generations to be heard.

Each movement of expansion – each revelation won through the soft unfolding of old pain – delivers a sense of purpose. Even the deeper areas of agony, when allowed to simply be as they are within our wider ecology, deliver a sense of reward. They reward us with their authenticity. This reward further releases us from the inner shackles of self-condemnation.

Nothing matters because it holds the sentient history of our sorrow. We hide within it when we are shocked, despised, thwarted and forsaken. These feelings matter, because they are the fuel within the alchemy that turns suffering into passion, passion into compassion and compassion into wisdom. Boredom matters, because it is an invitation for us to liberate depressed vitality, where our birth-right of passion has been thwarted, obligated, and controlled. It matters because it confuses us into believing there is no space on the inside and that we are creatures of limitation. It matters because embedded within its reptilian form is a living soul, and as its eye blinks in the light of consciousness, a fresh tear is falling.

When we soften our beliefs about the energy of boredom, and when we begin to realize that also nothing is something, and that something matters, we begin to walk different routes through the psyche. These routes will lead to the unmasking of our authentic sense of purpose, which will reveal a direction that cuts through the habits of pleasure-seeking and the avoidance of pain. Nothing is a door that when unlocked, reveals the potential for everything.

Passion

Suffering

Pain

Anger

Boredom

Numbness

13. A TRAGIC MAGIC

Passion and addiction

"No man ever steps in the same river twice."

HERACLITUS

We all need rhythm, repetition, and ritual in order to find structure in our lives. There is something natural and deeply relaxing in repeating patterns. There is a certain ease in the predictability of how we flow. We need patterns, because in a way we are an evolution of patterns. However, when the psyche is in conflict with itself, or when we have a conflict with certain aspects of experience, we lose balance in our grasping toward patterns as the only means through which to access that relief, release or inner peace. We start by being supported by them, then we begin to depend on them, then before long, we are exploiting them to keep other parts of the psyche down. Picture the classic movie image where someone gets into trouble, and immediately pours themselves a drink. They gulp back the alcohol, and the whole ritual of release, with a vengeance, and suddenly they feel empowered. In time, however, such addictive patterns are not empowering by disempowering. They give temporary relief with one hand, and with the other hand they cut us from the ground on which we stand. And then the psyche needs to split within itself again, from the inner addict. "I'm not addicted, it's just that I enjoy pornography, it gives me a feeling of freedom…" We refuse to be responsible for our destructive addictions partly, because of the social judgement that would be there if we own it, if we cross over the line from normal person to addict. The psyche of good society has literally split itself off from the society of addicts.

Addiction is a phenomenon that we tend to section in the dark alleyways of crack addicts, the over-lit halls of alcoholics anonymous, and the bleak web of losers and no-hopers. We are still far from recognizing the ubiquitous nature of addiction. If you say to me: "You are an addict!" I feel accused, condemned, dehumanized and threatened with banishment. The accusation of addiction has become a primal way to reject unwanted members from the tribe. Yet, increasingly, the tribe itself is bonding through choice patterns of addiction. We bond and find unity through the ritual of the pub at lunch time, the joint passes as an opener when friends gather, or the family cohesion depends on regular time spent invested in the next episode of a suspenseful TV series.

Addictive patterns are so much part of the state of the psyche, whether it is individual, collective, or ancestral, that its destructive form has been normalized, sanitized, and even prescribed. Addiction is described as those habits which are detrimental to our wellbeing, and when we look deeper into it, most of our collective habits are detrimental to our wellbeing, whether it is our addiction to fossil fuels, to electronics, or to the kind of wealth in which the value is all put in the car, mortgage and the pension.

In so many ways, our culture and conditioning are actively promoting addictive pathologies, at the same time as criminalizing the most chronic effects of this promotion.

Addiction becomes a suffering when we try to take something from the outside to fill the sense of lack on the inside. Our relationship with our true nature shifts. Whereas we could be fulfilled expressing and receiving qualities such as love, peace and release through the world, we now begin to depend on something in the world to give us those qualities. For example, we seek the chocolate to give us the sense of love, rather than loving the experience of chocolate.

Each time we try to fulfil our inner lack or to get a sense of belonging through an external object, we affirm the lack and end up feeling unfulfilled, lonely, and disconnected. Addiction begins to release when we remember ourselves as the source, or risk being the source. When we allow ourselves to be the one that is able to intuit, sense and explore the sense of lack, lack comes to life and we begin to remember ourselves as the source of all life.

There is a unifying principle found in our underlying, undifferentiated awareness that pervades all experience of any kind. Finding ourselves alive as this boundless awareness means that we undercut the compulsion of addictive patterns. We become less grasping, and our aversion is no longer anything other than a passing unpleasantness.

At this time, our conditioning and culture deeply advocate a reality of inner lack. This can come with a sense of not being enough, not having enough and not getting enough. We are inculcated with addictive tendencies from childhood. There is such a strength in this that we lose our natural context and the permission for our authentic spontaneity of movement. It can feel almost dissonant to say that something as simple as a daily walk in nature could be worth more for our wellbeing than psychiatric medication. Mindfulness (bringing attention to the natural rhythm of our breathing) is seen as fringe and slightly alternative (yes, being conscious of your breath is alternative). Yet, on the unsold fringes of our scientific literature, the evidence is there that such ways of being alive tremendously support our physical, psychological and collective wellbeing.

We are conditioned into a mindset of lack and self-condemnation, and this has begotten spirals of collective addictive behavior in which we are losing our direction and our sense of purpose. Yet still, the wheel of suffering turns.

What is the official definition of addiction?

> *"Addiction is a treatable, chronic medical disease involving complex interactions among brain circuits, genetics, the environment, and an individual's life experiences. People with addiction use substances or engage in behaviors that become compulsive and often continue despite harmful consequences. Prevention efforts and treatment approaches for addiction are generally as successful as those for other chronic diseases."* [4]

This standard definition states that addiction is caused by interactions between our brain circuits (read: conditioning); genetics (read: inherited trauma, stress responses and resilience); environment (read: education, culture, society, collective pathology); and individual life experiences (read: trauma). When you put it together, you find that the causes of addiction include just about everything – they are personal, collective, infective, contagious, inherited, historic and mental. All of these are mixed up together in a perfect storm – the storm that makes you an addict. But it is also the storm that makes you human.

Addiction is stated as a chronic medical disease, with holistic causes combining just about everything – biology, nature, and nurture. Something in the power, methodology and logic of addiction is so prevalent as to be part of our makeup, but it only becomes "addiction" when it is judged as bad or destructive to the wellbeing of the whole. Yet part of the badness and destructive effect of addiction is the result of the accusation of badness. Perhaps initially we sought out relief through certain rituals because we were in pain. When that habit is judged, the habit is made bad, but also our pain is made bad. The whole lot becomes "bad". We are becoming badness. The door of compassion closes.

After judging addiction as bad, we add to the addict the energy of badness, shame, and guilt, which has a potency that can demonize the core pain – giving it a resonance of evil. The accusation of being a perpetrator of harm accentuates the contraction and its unbearable resonance. As it is bad, destructive, and evil, we seek to control addiction and the addict. Yet when this control involves humiliation, domination, forced submission, repression, and oppression, when it has the resonance of prohibition, it further demonizes the pain. It repeats the original movement of contraction or trauma. It isolates and disconnects the person from their own center and vitality. In the words of addiction expert Scott Kiloby:

> *"Emphasizing "I should" and "I shouldn't" thoughts around an addictive substance or activity actually helps keep the addiction around, as it creates a sense of self that seems to have control. If control were truly the answer to addiction, humans wouldn't still be addicted, because everyone is already trying to control addictions. It isn't working."* [5]

Who decides between the "should" and "shouldn'ts" in our lives and according to what value system? Often the conditions we put on each other reflect the conditions we put on ourselves. These conditions are mostly born of fear and pain. They are based on avoiding that outcome or that pain. We seek to deal with pain rather than to heal it. To heal it, we need to find it, wherever it is hidden, and behind whatever it is hidden. Even when our deeper pain is hidden behind a bottle, inside an addict who appears as the stranger that we just can't forgive, our deeper need is to acknowledge that we are responsive to this pain. When we deny the pain, loss, or trauma within addictive patterns, and begin to dictate behaviors on others, we assume a standard without really standing for it, and then we begin a whole, circulating pandemic of shame and blame.

The habit of needing habits

How can we make this natural, rhythmic, ritualistic support system of repeating patterns of behavior work for us and not against us? How can we take the prison bars and find a scaffold for freedom in form – a ladder to the heavens?

An addictive tendency that brings wellbeing for the whole is clearly more needed than one that brings illness and death. How, then do we harness the power of addiction for the greater good?

> "The difference between passion and addiction is that between a divine spark and a flame that incinerates."
>
> Gabor Maté

Not by denying it, but by riding its power. The pressure, compulsion, vitality, and transformative power within the movement of passion resembles the addictive mechanism, only here there is an orientation toward the wellbeing of others through which the biochemistry of reward is spontaneously arising. We can take the passion but leave the battle for the bottle behind.

What is an addict? Here, we see the definition is not just covering substance abuse (food, alcohol, drugs), but also behaviors. What is behind both substance and behavior is the factor of compulsion. Our actions are compelled by a force which is greater than the authority that says we should not. To be compelled is to be forced, so addiction is when we are forced into a certain pattern. Yet the addict is often treated as the one having the compulsion – they are compulsive – rather than the one that is compelled. There is a split into two – a war going on between good and bad – which delivers a kind of stress and distress that seeks relief, one way or another.

Within this compulsion is the intense energetic charge of pain. Empowering addiction is that sense of unbearable agony in the psyche which is at once deeply true and utterly disavowed. We find that torment in the areas where we lose our compassion, where we break- down, where the resonance is an ongoing torture and is therefore unforgivable. In the words of Gabor Maté:

> *"Not all addictions are rooted in abuse or trauma, but I do believe they can all be traced to painful experience. A hurt is at the centre of all addictive behaviours. It is present in the gambler, the Internet addict, the compulsive shopper and the workaholic. The wound may not be as deep and the ache not as excruciating, and it may even be entirely hidden—but it's there. As we'll see, the*

effects of early stress or adverse experiences directly shape both the psychology and the neurobiology of addiction in the brain.[6]

The addictive substance or behavior is the one thing that delivers a momentary sense of wholeness, or freedom from conflict. The divisive nature of the ongoing war is also found in the splitting into competing external authorities: the authority that says you must not drink that whisky, and the authority that says that you must. Either way, the whisky is the issue, so it always wins. The substance becomes the common ground between the "should" and the "shouldn't". At least with the whiskey, we move beyond conflict. In whiskey, we are one.

The standard definition of addiction continues with the stipulation that these compulsions are those that have "harmful consequences". Notice the judgement. Judgement heaps the energy of badness on whatever it is that you are compelled to do. It puts badness on your compulsion. This badness includes the vibrations of shame, guilt, and abuse. Your addiction has consequences, so now you are not a victim, but a perpetrator, so we can add cruelty to the list. There is a visceral threat of evil in it, and that evil is pushed toward the addict with his generational, environmental, cognitive, personal, brain mess of perpetual badness. This badness is constantly refilled by the scorn of others, so the addict now also suffers extra helpings of loneliness, isolation, condemnation, and despair. The self-destruction drive-thru goes turbo.

At this stage, let us breathe and take in a timely reminder: we are all prone to addiction. We are all addicts. We are addicted to being stupefied by our smartphones and to shutting down socially with social media. We sit stunned in our addiction to the news and to movie channels of terror, suspense, and ridicule. We are addicted to fast food, slow thought, and chemical killers of pain. We are compelled into easier ways to shop, lazier ways to survive, and cheaper ways to ignore the itching questions of our own life force. We toast the destruction of the planet with petrol and fly everywhere while bellowing smoke across the oceans. We are compelled to attend to sexist abuse, tyrants, war, atrocity and injustice and we revel in it, as long as it is far out there, away from our private, separate inner world.

We are addicted because the horror somehow makes us feel alive. We are addicted because in some forsaken precinct of the soul, we feel slightly less alone. And when we are done fumigating the soul through projection on "the world", we re-engage with lame small talk and grandiose blame.

We are addicted to being "someone" and to losing no one. We drown ourselves in casual desire and snort the toxins of gender hate to spice things up. We lie and we buy ourselves into prisons of choice. We are all addicted and despite the harmful consequences, we have sorely neglected and denied our inborn passion for life.

If that last paragraph of holy rant makes you angry, let it. This is your own intimate passion on the rise.

If, for a moment, we could take the sense of badness out of our collective state of addiction, and instead be curious about this tendency to seek wellbeing in all the wrong places, then we begin to find a middle way to wholeness. What we know for sure, between our sorry state as addicts and our unfulfilled state as good citizens, is that both are seeking wellbeing. Yet wellbeing is not a stagnant state of "good-ism". It is a tremendously powerful magnetic force. It is an impulse that runs through everyone and everything – from the source of me, directly to the source of you. It is where the point of me finds the point of you. Wellbeing seeks itself through manifold form. It is unstoppable. It is right here: where we are one.

That which can never be lost

You can fleece an individual of everything, but you will never take away her incessant search for wellbeing. The force within the passage between one soul and another through the physical wilderness of creative possibility is what we call passion. Wellbeing awakens, meets, and unifies through all forms of life through the power of passion.

We have been frustrated in our natural, passionate manifestation. According to the stated definition of addiction, by genetic, mental, environmental, and personal patterns. In the previous chapter we looked into boredom – how the energy of passion has been frozen, numbed and disabled through congealed areas of insensitivity in the psyche. Yet boredom alone cannot block passion, only part of it. We still crave release, purpose, reward, and fulfilment. We still fiercely long to be part of the whole. The life force of the whole universe, sourced in infinite abundance, is putting a perpetual pressure for movement, manifestation, and freedom in form. There is a sense of pending combustion, as the pressure of unreleased passion builds up inside ourselves and we begin to feel deeply uncomfortable within the limitations of our own skin. We are longing to shed the skin, to grow, to live, to love and to return to naturalness. Even the patterns, plans, agendas and prohibitions and the whole strength of collective man cannot ultimately dumb this pressure of passion down.

One effect of the contraction of passion into the density of boredom is that of repetition. We start to cling to the known, the safe and the predictable. This shows up as reflexes and habits. These reflexes and habits are formed, like the boredom, according to the principle of attaining pleasure and avoiding pain, of feeling good and not bad. But the freedom of experience depends on confrontations with the unknown. These confrontations make us nervous, and we try to stabilize ourselves into known, predictable patterns. These patterns include patterns of behavior, patterns of reactivity, patterns of intake, and patterns of expression. Our habits show up as eating habits, drinking habits, habitual expressions and habitual organizations of time, space, and movement. Some of our addictive, predictable, compulsive behaviors can become deeply boring to ourselves and others. The core of passion is still throbbing behind the crust of the personality, wanting to break loose.

Passion in naturalness brings direction, unconditional reward, fulfillment, and the sense of purpose. Although it relieves us of the internal pressure to manifest, it actually increases the vitality that is available to manifest even more. It energizes us, from the cellular level, easing the heart and opening the mind. It gives voice to all that need to speak, while listening with the ears of eternity to all that needs to be heard. As it moves with compassion, it longs to meet itself, passing over the perimeters of separation, unconfused by passages of isolation.

But sometimes, it seems impossible to come there, and this is where addictive patterns get a grip. Feeling bored or numbed down within ourselves, separated from the authenticity of our own life-force and bereft of purpose, we seek relief on the outside. We trade the long game of the soul's manifestation for the short game of passing personal gratification, and we trade our heroes for ghosts.

That external crutch – that substance, relationship, behavior, or activity – does bring a sense of relief. The energy is at least on the move. It feels purposeful for a while. It gives a passing sense of reward. Dopamine is released in the brain and there are moments of bliss. But the effect is short lived. We fall back into the dense "nothing" of the inner world.

As our tolerance to the substance increases, so does our intolerance to states of boredom. We reach further and further outside of ourselves for more. Yet we always seem to end up with less. We start to hunger, for ever greater quantities to get that moment of bliss. But the more we reach out, the more we get the thundering sense of absolutely nothing on the inside. We feel unbearably hollow. The speed of gain and loss accelerates as we spiral further and further away from our seemingly coreless center through increasing degrees of dependency. You can't trust life, but you can trust the next joint to make you feel a little better.

All of physical life and evolution is based on learning through patterns of repetition. Our days and nights, our bodies, and the psyche, are all orchestrated through rhythms of sacred ritual. Even our thoughts and the language we speak are made up of repeated encodings, consensual expressions, and habitual blind-spots. That is partly why each chapter of this book begins with a common and vaguely absurd idiom.

Addiction is when these rituals become ritualistic slavery, where we are no longer empowered but subjugated, where we are no longer manifesting but possessed, where we are no longer expanding in wellbeing, but are held hostage by whole gangs of second-hand sufferings.

Passion, like poetry and great literature, will disrupt patterns. It will form new patterns to fly with and will junk the ones that held it back. Passion arises from the field of infinite potential as an alchemical energy that can pull the angel out of the devil's heart and the victory out of demolition. It is that power that can set us free so that we are no longer enslaved to patterns, but rather, our patterns work for us. Yet to step out of the conditions of suffering, we need to put down our precious attempts to survive in separation from the whole. This means unleashing the passion to be of service to the greater wellbeing.

When we stop the behavior, or withdraw the substance, we can be faced with implosion into the hell realms of castrated, bored, horrified energy that have built up within us. Part of this can be the energy of pure self-destruction, the zone of suicidal energy. Here, there is a blizzard of violence acting against itself due to the impossibility of expressing such a voltage into the world. The urge to outer violence (to cut yourself to cut a way through) is backfiring in a blizzard of inner violence, where murderer and victim entwine. It is the loneliest, most desperate space, and it would be so worthwhile to realize that we all – everyone of us – share it. It is a blizzard of conflicting sensations; it does not define the sky.

Around this hell we will find those core wounds and those emotional structures of pain and humiliation that initially caused the lock down. All we need is to let ourselves be passionate enough to let them breathe. When we find the passion in the process, the process releases still more passion. When we allow our sensitivity, it begins to make sense. The deeper sense of purpose in the experience awakens. Compassion spontaneously arises to meet the revelation of that which has been denied.

Even if we have no memory of a signature event, or no known cause for our distress, we need not falter. The sense of being distressed is its own validation. The need for justification is part of the paradigm that created the block in the first place. It rapidly squanders us into the consensual compulsion to split the world into right and wrong.

Liberation comes with a shift in attitude to suffering. When distress is allowed to be here, and we are allowed to feel it in its purity, expanding as the pure awareness around and through it, it will no longer obstruct our purpose, but will become part of it. The healing power of passion is arising, lighting up all that it touches with pristine innocence. Passion will create and destroy our conditioning. It will reinvent our rituals. Bringing instant fulfillment that can never be lost, it is a gamechanger of the psyche that will reward us with pleasure, pain, loss, and gain, all the way to kingdom come.

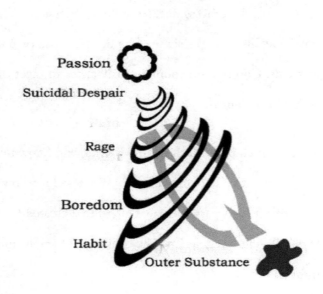

14. LONGING TO LIVE

Passion and the secret formulas of longing

"Your calling my name is my reply. Your longing for me is my message to you."

RUMI

When we move into how addiction actually feels – how it resonates within our felt sense – we find a craving. The craving is beyond hunger and beyond thirst. We crave something more formless than food, drink, or any substance. What is it that we are really craving? When you put the "stuff" aside, what are we truly longing for? Where does the longing come from?

What we crave, through substance, behavior, or attachment, is to come to a certain kind of experience, an experience of completion. We are longing for wholeness or fulfillment through reunion. To find reunion, our longing passes over and through the energetic stuff of the separate self and extends into the outer world.

Do you remember how in Chapter 7 we discuss the blurry line between the words "suffering" and "experience"? For us addicts, the first living intervention is our own intervention with the suffering nature of experience. We try to get a grip of that line between pleasure and pain. We want the pleasant or positive sensations, but not the negative. We resist suffering by seeking to control the nature of experience – recruiting the effects of outer entities for the purpose. But as we pointed out earlier, resistance to life is futile and is its own kind of suffering. It can only ever buy as some time to process experience later. The deep suffering of many addicts is that "later" never comes, and we then lose ourselves in a repeating cycle of craving for the next antidote to the pain caused by the diminished effect of the earlier antidote. The sense of purpose is hijacked by the next fix, as the experience we crave boils down to one set of antidotal sensations: relief, release, and reprieve.

Sometimes the atmosphere of addiction merges with the atmosphere of insanity, the atmosphere of trauma, and the atmosphere of criminality. In reaching out for private relief from personal suffering, we can with time find ourselves adrift in an ocean of resonant pain – a vast, collective field of disimpassioned despair. For some of us, that atmosphere feels like home. It is got sense of truth in it. It vibrates with the darker inner secret – that condemned and rejected suffering deep on the inside – that same suffering that spurred the addiction in the first place.

Here, in the bereaved bedlam of society's rejects, there are whole communities of lost and forgotten souls. These are subcultures, where anyway true nature lives and breathes. As with every community, even here, there is a resource of unity. Compassion abounds. Because of the permission given to the core of suffering and rage, it can feel for some to be more truthful and freer than all the socially conformed pretenses that play out above ground. The longing for reunion, through connection is even stronger than the addiction. Communities form at street level. There is a solidarity in being free beneath the level of social striving and control.

Think of someone who you consider socially acceptable, clean of harmful addictions, and well-adjusted to society. You meet him on the street. How real is the exchange? When you seek eye contact, or true connection, what happens? Now picture a homeless junky, coming to you for spare change. Seek eye contact with her. What do you see? Is the need for connection met? Who blinks first? Who is more afraid? What happens within your inner world? Can you feel the awakeness, and the stirring of compassion?

Nondual Passion

Sooner or later, whether through the inner dive into the perceptive source of who we are, or through the outer reaches of addiction, we will all return to the vital source of our own origination. If not on the inside, then through the eye of another. If not in the light, then in the depths of our own darkest hour. If not by trial, then by error. We will all unfold as the purpose of suffering which is passion. This is our destiny, if not now, then now.

The pain experienced at the intimate core of ourselves isn't "other" than the pain experienced "out there" in the world. It is a sentient vibration within our conscious awareness. Only later the thoughts come to partition what is "here" and what is "there", what is "near" and what is "far" and what is "mine" and what is "yours".

If there is a need to meet the core of our suffering on the inside, and this is thwarted, then we will meet it out in the world. Because in the field of pure resonance, outside is also inside and inside is outside. The only divider is the mental arbitration of the perimeters of the separate self. If our purpose is to allow the power of passion, then that power will arise, with violence, fire, and brimstone (if needed), to clear the passage for the soul.

The word violence literally stems in the word "via" meaning a way or passage. If our deeper need is to realize compassion, and we close our hearts to our inner scream, then we will find compassion on the outside, through hearing the scream of others. We may control the imaginative distancing of the experience, but we may not ultimately escape the experience itself. We can run, but we cannot hide, and if for a while we do hide, the deeper yearning of our soul will never be denied. It will show up as fresh as day from within even the darkest hide-outs of consciousness.

Part of our deeper individual purpose and responsibility is to find the courage to break the patterning of addiction. This happens when we allow a shift from a state of victimhood to responsibility. This shift comes when the louder voices of consensus from the social field lose the power to distract us from our deeper yearning. It is a shift in direction, from looking for individual reward outside of ourselves, to opening a willingness to share all benefit and to be of service to the whole. In this, patterns of addiction lose their stranglehold, as we reconnect with an area of ourselves in which there is no limitation. Patterns, repetition and cycles become attuned with the good of the whole, and stress decreases. Our whole physiology begins to relax as a reprogramming occurs in which reflexes, habits and patterns are softer, more flexible and adaptable according to the depth of need in real time. Our conditioning evolves from the binary software of suffering to the full scope of formulas arising and expressing through unlimited potential.

There is a deep need for us all to begin to reverse engineer the pathology of addiction within our collective conditioning. This means that we do a U-turn back to center, walking the way of the addict but now in reverse. Rather than reaching out, we reach in. A whole new journey opens up within ourselves.

The magic in the felt sense of longing

It starts with the craving. Not the object that is craved for, but the felt sense of craving – feeling it in the body, getting a visceral sense of the lack within it. That is where we are going next: to the lack. This sense of lack appears as an empty wine cabinet but is sourced in a far more profound universal sense – in pure space or emptiness.

Yet if it were just emptiness it would not be so dreadful. It is emptiness with horror in it; emptiness with menace; emptiness with the rapturous pain of separation. It is unformed and boundless, and it feels unbearable. The sense of lack can feel like an abscess or true nature within an even colder absence; the abject horror within abandonment; the torturous wasting and waiting within neglect; the shaking sorrow within the forsaken. It threatens to possess us, just as it breathes out aversion. How could we not seek distraction? The sense of lack isn't lacking, it is full of every variety of agony around the primal splitting open of the universe. It claims god-like authority and omnipotence.

If we stay with this sense of lack, even in small, local ways, we can explore it as a passing sensation, however, and not as an absolute reality or bottom line of being. It is even possible to resource the very space we have been dreading. When we take time and space to allow the unbearable sense of lack to breathe, a differentiation occurs.

Here, there is pure, empty space, and over here, there is horror. Here, there is a living, powerful stillness, and here, there are waves of sorrow. Here, there is a vast silence, and there are the muted yet piercing screams of despair. There is this and there is that. With time, space, and sentient discernment, we can break the wedlock between them and disarm the toxic association of emptiness with human agony.

The lack is no longer only toxic, even though there is some toxicity around the sense of lack. Just as pollution from our factories cannot define the sky, the emptiness within the lack is not defined by our history of pain. Emptiness is not poisonous, and poison does not define it. It is a pure, unadulterated, continuous, and primal resource of all manifestation. This emptiness is in every living thing, and in the space between things. It is in our sensory ability, allowing us to hear music, smell a flower and see a sunset. It is not our worst nightmare, but the ubiquitous, all-pervading, existential spaciousness that allows our minds to know, our feelings to flow, and all things to grow. It is not the destroyer of life but the facilitator that makes all experience possible, giving the existential permission even to time, space, and frequency. Being in the sense of lack and the liberation of the sense of lack, we might begin to feel something stirring. This deep stirring is occurring at a depth beyond the scream of pain. Our craving for relief is now showing up as a longing for life. It is as if something is awakening the soul. There is a stirring, a yearning, a reaching out, a kind of prayer arising from the mysterious core of ourselves directed to the endless, mysterious expanse of the whole. Our whole being is inclined towards communion.

How should we meet the challenge of this endless unmet need, this depth of longing? Would we now turn again into the world and distract ourselves, looking for that which will make it quiet? How would we know what we are searching for? How do we find the source of our longing, except through a deeper passage into the core of lack? For at the core of the sense of lack, our longing is unfolding.

Within the lack there is a longing, and within the longing there is a missing, and within the missing there is a sentient memory of that which has been lost. How could we miss something if we didn't know what it is? How could we be longing for something if it has been forgotten? How could our heart be aching for something if it doesn't remember how it feels?

Within the missing, deep within the felt sense of longing, there is the felt sense of that which we are longing for. When we agree to feel the longing, we also feel the fulfillment of the longing. When we get a feeling connection with the which we are longing for, we begin to experience it.

The liberated emptiness of lack will permit this resonance, to move through mental objections and outcries from the injured sense of lack that it cannot be there. It is there. It is here right behind and within the existential core of ourselves – the potential for the fulfillment of our cravings, longings, prayers and purpose. We have followed the intimate trail of our feelings back to the living core of unique passion. We have stepped back from addiction to craving, from craving to lack, from lack to longing, from longing to reunion and from reunion to passion.

Longing is like a prayer at the core of our essential manifestation. It is a prayer in which the quality deep inside the individual seeks to manifest, and to come to life as beauty. It is a prayer that when given voice is always resonantly answered.

It can be felt in the way that the inner light reaches toward the outer light. It is the life within emanating as a whole living universe. Is that inner, inalienable freedom, seeking the myriad fields of expression through outer freedom. It is the unseasoned, unstoppable care of our being expanding into the vast unfettered care of the universe. It is a prayer, which like the purest of questions, already contains its answer. It is the purpose that has long been restless inside, where something is unresolved, something is needed, that starts to move in service to the purpose of the whole. It is the passion arising from within, urgently, immediately, needing confluence with the passionate, evolutionary flow of the whole.

When we let the passion at the core of ourselves resonate, then we resonate passion, through all layers of form. That is because the all-prevailing emptiness surrounds, underlies, and is interspersed through every tiny string of physical life.

When we unlock the passion at the core of the longing, then passion is untethered, and it resonates through all dimensions of time and space. When we allow the passion to vibrate out of the heart of emptiness, then every fiber of our being vibrates with passion. When the need hidden deep inside the longing, the music of our deepest purpose, begins to sing, an orchestra of angels are swaying in harmony. A universal passion is on the move from inside out, reaching from the source of wellbeing into the myriad manifestations of life, searching and delighting to meet itself along the way.

The longing in this infinite source of power is the passion for life, and it harmonizes with the passion in all forms of life, manifesting as the path-breaking deeper purpose of the whole of life.

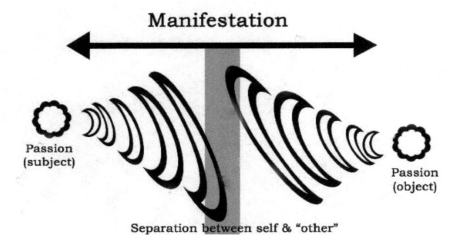

15. CREATE AN UPROAR

A destructive, creative process

"Art is not a handicraft, it is the transmission of feeling the artist has experienced."

LEO TOLSTOY

There can be a certain blind arrogance when we assume that the manifest potential of our physical universe is defined by what we can perceive through our physical senses, and the limitations of these organs. Yet trust in known science is based on this materialist belief. This is especially poignant when we consider how our structures of belief so often define the limits of our perception. We only see what we believe it is possible to see. We only hear what we want to hear. We only feel what we think matters.

We are caught in a paradox of perception. We can't believe in something until we can see it, but we can't physically see it, until we believe it could be there.

Beliefs have hijacked the perceptive power of consciousness, especially in relation to the sensuous mystery of the unknown. In this, beliefs have a complex relationship with passion – which is the spontaneous manifestation, facilitation, and expression of the unknown source potential through our bodies, hearts and minds.

This is where our creative power cuts the middle way. Beliefs are about protection, control, preservation, structure, and safety. They slow down and restrain the rapid influx of information into consciousness. Too much change, or too much differentiation threatens the stability of the whole. Where disintegration is threatened, beliefs are tools of integration.

When we engage in a creative process – giving form to affliction or irresolution – we simultaneous ride on the power of passion and of belief. The two conflicting forces – acceleration and deceleration – become one in attuned transmission. Through our creativity, the deeper, structural power of mind aligns with the elemental power of passion. The progeny is then offered to the whole in a movement of transmission, service, or expression. All experience is sooner or later shared experience.

Let's study for a moment how it feels to open a creative window. We are active in our intention, and in the opening, but after that, the movement is one of facilitation. We permit the passage of source energy through us. We allow inspiration from the unknown. We open the window and wait for the exact resonance to arise – a resonance that strikes a chord of expression through body, heart and mind. While "doing" something creative might be a way to open the creative window, the true creativity is in the flow – the passage – of source energy into form. This is where heaven comes to earth, or spiritual energy fuses with denser energies, and a healing process unfurls. The creative offering is full of quality and is energized by pure consciousness. It alleviates internal pressure while elevating the whole.

When we allow a nondual quality to resonate unconditionally within the field of conscious awareness, regardless of the state of suffering within the psyche, we enter a creative process. When peace pulsates, regardless of the stuttering of war and surrender, a creativity comes forward proffering possibilities for progress. When love vibrates, even when hatred hunts out sacrifice, the voltage in the violence is deflated. When beauty bestows her charms, how our vulgarity and inner ugliness melts in a unison of wonder.

Our creativity is the vehicle in which our passion rides. The qualities of our true nature, arising through passion, cut a passage of middle ways in a creative process of evolution.

Yet our beliefs are conditioned to pit our pain against our true nature. Where we are in pain, for example, we cannot experience bliss; where we are in love, we cannot experience hatred; we cannot experience our truth, as long as there are lies; or we cannot feel peace, as long as there are wars. Our beliefs put true nature in conflict with the conflicted parts of the psyche. It's *either-or* and mutually exclusive. True nature is a bargaining chip that we could lose in the war against suffering.

Our beliefs have been formed in the duality of opposing opposites, and their deeper need is to evolve into the perception of collaborating pairs. This evolution is a creative process. Where there is an attitude of collaboration, as well as competition, creativity arrives, and passion thrives. Under this evolutionary principle, even competition can be collaborative, just as collaboration can be competitive, all is in service to the evolution or healing of the whole.

Part of our evolution is the evolution of the brain. As a physical entity bridging mind and body, the brain has been trained to protect, survive and to make sense of vast amounts of information. One way we do this is through our beliefs. Yet beliefs so often cause passion to back-fire, confuse our direction, and bottleneck our creativity.

If we go into the core meaning of the word, we find that to "believe" is to fall in love with a form. The root word "lieve" is derived from its Proto-Indo-European root leubh, meaning: "to care, desire, love." This means that the very mental apparatus through which we structure our reality – our systems of belief – are in naturalness orchestrations of love. They come to life through the feeling connection. They decide on our point of view and the general orientation of the heart and soul. With a mission of love, our beliefs direct where and how we resource ourselves: they can turn us toward Jerusalem or toward the magnificence of a mushroom, as a means to resource the soul. They are part of how we orientate our purpose in a vast universe.

When there is a conflict in feeling, such as when we hate and love a person at the same time, trouble arises. Our thoughts try to make sense of it – offering beliefs as precepts and conclusions that seem to bridge the gap. For example: "All men are naturally promiscuous", a belief that uses trust to bridge love and suspicion of men – you can trust all men to be promiscuous, so I can still love my treacherous brother.

In time, beliefs get less and less conscious, controlling perception from the shadows, often disconnected from sensitivity, and feeling, and showing up as soulless dogma. As they enter us through repetition and habit, becoming part of our autonomous physiology, damaging beliefs can assume the furniture of home. They become assumed forms of limitation which are normalized, weaponized, and unquestioned.

The heart – and the power of universal love that moves through it – is radically free. Our beliefs are born as tools to serve this love, they were never meant to be the structures through which love is denied. Our beliefs are born to work for the qualities of our true nature, not against them.

In naturalness, beliefs are mental tools to support our manifestation and the uprising of passion, not to repress it. This repression originating in old, disembodied beliefs can lead to long term depression. It can be delightful and surprising, sometimes, to have a belief broken. It can be a relief to dispel a belief – as an unbridled power of love can again shine through the cracks in our nominal reality.

Yet at the same time, beliefs are protective structures. They were born in reaction to extreme experience to facilitate trust, balance, and safety. They are often our defenses against danger and coping strategies for a hostile world. This means that when they weaken or break, we often face that very threat of suffering or pain that they blocked. They are associated with the pain, they are attached, so when the beliefs rattle, that old pain also screeches. These rattling screeching sounds of distress can sound the alert to tighten the chains and secure the locks on the mind. We are caught in a cycle, until we find the creative space in which it is possible to allow a change in attitude.

Attitude can steer our beliefs in a beneficial direction. Our attitudes are part of our inclination of consciousness, or the way we perceive things. They affect what we see and how we see it. Like tinted sunglasses on the eyes of the soul, our attitudes have an all-pervasive effect on how we perceive reality and therefore on the nature of our experience. Attitudes of consciousness influence the quality of our experience.

When there is a foreboding attitude, we will find danger everywhere and we will cope with this by closing down perception and reducing sensitivity. Where there is an attitude of a nondual quality, for example, passion, our consciousness invites the expansion of quality around and through us. This is because the qualities of our true nature are integral to consciousness and are powerful accelerators of consciousness.

A passionate attitude will lead to passionate thoughts, passionate beliefs, the attraction toward passion in others, and an invitation to passion extended toward others. This quality feedback further expands the resonance of passion within consciousness. Rewarded by the sense of wellbeing, the inclination toward passion is further developed, from the cells of the body, through the nerve system, all the way to the neural networks of the brain. We evolve through all layers to be able to channel higher and higher frequencies of passion.

But are we able to allow passion when it seems to threaten the structures of our beliefs? What is our attitude to passion in suffering and the suffering in passion? Can we let suffering be part of the passion? Whether victim or perpetrator, how do we deal with the darker side, the more horrific aspects of experience? Do we deflate and become purposeless, settling for a general sense of lostness? Or could these subterranean vital passages of pain be our validation as blood-giving co-creators of the whole earth? Could it be that this conflict of opposites at cause within suffering is that which sparks a flame of passion to light up our whole world?

We always have a choice to return immediately, without hesitation, out of the wilderness of belief structures and into the clarity and inclusivity of our true nature. We are free to navigate between deceleration through resistance, and acceleration through the passion within the pain. This choice has everything to do with our creativity. It is out of this space that there is a collaboration between mind, psyche and body, which allows an opening of the creative window, to let the full mystery of the universe express intimately and uniquely through you. To move with creativity is to co-create the experience of the whole. It is to be a direct observer participant in the unfolding creation of the universe, and to be in direct service to the whole. All this is implicit and explicit revelation made possible through the nondual quality of passion.

At the core of the creative principle of the physical universe there is this friction, and this pain is the alchemical substance within the passion to evolve, heal, serve, express, and share the source qualities of our true nature. In allowing this, we remember ourselves as the deep authority, the origin of truth, and the creator of all forms of experience. We have a profound individual purpose: to allow the unique forms of true nature to manifest through us in unity with the whole.

Unique, alive and in unity

Creativity is not just about art, it is also about innovation, the skills of creative problem solving, and the movement beyond the limitations of binary mind. In the famous words of Steve Jobs, founder of Apple Computers:

> *"Here's to the crazy ones, the misfits, the rebels, the troublemakers, the round pegs in the square holes... the ones who see things differently – they're not fond of rules. You can quote them, disagree with them, glorify or vilify them, but the only thing you can't do is ignore them because they change things... they push the human race forward, and while some may see them*

as the crazy ones, we see genius, because the ones who are crazy enough to think that they can change the world, are the ones who do."[7]

Our evolutionary human endeavor is to bring heaven to earth and earth to heaven, and this is a creative process fired by passion. We are universal co-creators, individually answerable to the opportunity of our unique manifestation. In this, the deeper responsibility is in allowing our creativity – in being humble enough in our personalities to admit the godliness of the inner creator.

Through creativity, passion manifests: suffering becomes service; impermanence becomes beauty; terror becomes awe; and annihilation becomes unity.

Creativity opens us to the unknown aspects of experience, allowing whatever is needed from the zero-point field to come to life within awareness, and to be transmitted into the world. It is a whole movement of transformation in which the insufferable becomes sufferable and reveals its essence of beauty and truth.

When conditions allow, that which was excluded, unacceptable and violating is aroused from the core of the body and begins to express, through music, art, and literature. Suddenly, there is love infiltrating the pain; beauty revealed in the loss; and purpose unfolding even out of despair. What was denied is revealed, what was banished comes home, and what was isolated becomes the very means through which we touch one another.

The creative principle is innate to the quality of passion. It is there at the birth of the whole physical universe and in the birth of each moment in time. Yet creation is a destructive process. It involves collision, breakage, splintering and rupture. It is full of pain. Everything that is born must just as surely die. Each moment of arrival is a moment departing. Change, impermanence, and loss are definitive parameters to our being here in freedom. Without this movement, there would be no creation and no life, and this is literally inconceivable.

We are in a process of remembering that our beliefs are here to be of service to the whole, not to protect us from it. In this transformation of how we use beliefs, one of the first entanglements to show up will be in the belief that creation is the opposite of destruction. That creation is "good", and destruction is "bad". In this belief, we lose the power of passion, as our creativity loses half its motor.

When we resist destruction, the psyche gets demoted as a creator and it becomes a controller. But the energy of destruction does not go away, it just gets diverted. Commanded to keep control, we are compelled to destroy that which cannot be controlled. One of the most pressing energies to control is this destructive, wild passion of true nature. We seek to destroy the destruction that is in it. Under pressure of the same passion, we will even seek creative ways to destroy destruction. Anything goes, as long as we are in control. Yet this strategic controller, a mosaic of coping mechanisms, hardly offers a shadow of who we truly are and who we are becoming. It lost the feeling connection and where we lose feeling, we close the senses, and where our senses are closed, life seems senseless. In time, this senselessness becomes pointlessness and pointlessness become meaninglessness. Disimpassioned, we lose all purpose. What is the sense in singing a song?

Every moment of manifestation is sustained through a natural balance of creation and destruction. Take the cells within the body, for example, if there is an overdrive of cell creation, we get a tumor; if there is an overdrive of cell destruction, we get neurodegeneration. This balance, this intelligence, that has the discernment to know when to be born and when to die, is what brings wellbeing to the whole. It is at the core of our passion. Also, at the depth of the methodology of creation, destruction and passion is the offering to the wellbeing of the whole. Where some cells act in isolation, all the cells suffer.

The keyword therapeutically is movement. When we acknowledge the uniquely formed pain at the core of ourselves, then we can give it space. Already with that spaciousness, we can bring an unconditional attitude – such as an attitude of softness or curiosity. As the pain decontracts and comes to life, it seeks a voice, it needs to express, it wants to move and to be transmitted. The creative process is a key facilitator in allowing it to take form into the universe of the living. This offering and release, from the inside-out, resonates with truth. It is always of service to the whole.

Creation happens in the moment of destruction. New expressions of life emerge through the gap where older forms have split open. When we become one with the "other", we blend as a new form of unity and we destroy the separate entity. When we split from that unity, we create new forms of life.

Imagine you are a seed of pure potential, buried deep inside the earth. You are silently but stealthily expanding within your shell. There is an incremental unfolding. You begin to press up against the barriers and to intuit a warm glow of light. Then, that moment comes. Without wanting it, you are breaking open the shell that has been your sanctuary of growth. It is splitting apart, and it feels like the end of the world, all known reality is ruptured, and you reach through the gap toward the light. Your body has broken apart, but you are still here, no longer a grain, but a shoot of life, aroused into a vast dimension of space, reaching up and stretching outward. Through passion that moves beyond any split between creation and destruction, new life is arising. You are creating a whole tree within a lineage of trees. Your purpose is unfolding the unique expression of the universal tree that was always there, deep within the shell, within the seed, within the zygote, in the vast space of pure potential, out of a star that shines with the purest light of purpose.

16. QUALITY CONFLICTS

When passion conflicts with other nondual qualities

"Against stupidity the very gods themselves contend in vain."

FRIEDRICH SCHILLER

Students of Nondual Therapy and readers of this book are in an evolutionary process of discovering the myriad qualities of true nature, which are inseparable from the qualities of consciousness. As we explored in the introduction, these qualities are abundant, unconditional, timeless, and infinite. They never get lost and can never be injured. All that happens is that our connection with them changes to denser forms. For example, our connection with purity shows up as the frozen purity which is shame; or our connection with freedom shows up as the frozen freedom which is slavery. The quality was never lost, it just became contracted, and it is waiting to decontract.

When our consciousness touches this energetic contraction, we sense the suffering of the manifest quality. For example, when we become conscious of guilt, we sense the suffering of innocence. We begin to suffer our innocence. This suffering of innocence can only be sensed because of the pure innocence within the consciousness. Only innocence can sense guilt. If we were guilty to the core, we couldn't feel it. This guilt is made of contracted innocence, and there is an energetic recognition.

In this way, consciousness is a catalytic healer of the psyche. Consciousness contains the living templates of the qualities of true nature in unadulterated form, and the touch of consciousness is an invitation for contracted energies to melt back to source. In the words of quantum physicist David Bohm: "Universe consists of frozen light."

Within the unified field, there is creation, and creation is a process of differentiation in which the implicit field of infinite possibility becomes explicit. A core dimension of differentiation is that in which we sense the nondual qualities or qualities of true nature. These include powerful energies such as love, peace, freedom, care, and purity. These qualities are an inseparable, interdependent orchestra of infinite variety. In naturalness, each quality is a portal to a dimension in which all the rest live. There is a vast harmony and ultimately one recognizable, potent, all-powerful, all-inclusive sweetness that defies definition, but is called by the Buddhists Mettā (often translated as "loving kindness").

Sometimes, the psyche will block one quality at the expense of another. It will hold them apart in a state of competition, as if one quality threatens the other. For example, the quality of freedom could be taken as incompatible with the quality of care; the quality of belonging as incompatible with the quality of truth; or the quality of peace as incompatible with the quality of passion.

As part of its controlling mechanism, as a strategy to survive, the psyche splits itself into subparts in which the flow of information is broken down in a field of conflict or suffering. The part of me that cares for my children, for example, might demand the sacrifice of the part of me that needs to move in freedom. The part of me that is loving, might demand the sacrifice of the part of me that is truthful, (or vice versa).

Healing comes when we are able to blend the two qualities that have been polarized in the psyche. For example, let's imagine there is a conflict between passion and care. When we find the passion in care, what happens? When we find the care in our passion, what happens? What had seemed mutually exclusive refines and becomes truer. Where parts of the psyche were breaking connection, a whole new flow of information exchange starts up. It is entirely possible that the resource of one quality will help liberate the contraction in the other. Our care, for example, becomes much more unconditional, genuine, precise, and empowered when it has passion in it.

In this psychological minefield of quality conflict, passion is a family black sheep, and is often a forerunner for sacrifice. This is ironic, because passion is the quality with the elixir that can awaken all the other qualities form anywhere and everywhere. For example, the quality of love might falter at a mass grave, but passion will not; passion will unlock the love from its conditions. The quality of care might falter if it needs to destroy, but passion will not. Passion will unlock the care from its conditions. In the words of Viktor Frankl:

> *"It is not freedom from conditions, but it is freedom to take a stand toward the conditions."*

When we consider all the reasons why not to be passionate, we will find the quality conflicts around passion. Perhaps we deny our passion, because then we would feel devoid of care? Passion, after all, can seem egocentric, arrogant, inconsiderate and risks being hurtful to others. Passion can be destructive, and caring people preserve; they do not destroy. To be passionate, we need to be careless, right? We need to throw all worries to the wind, and just go for it.

But how would it be to be passionate in our care? How would it be to care deeply for our passion? Could we imagine a way in which passion is care and care is passion? Can we get a sense of the process of liberated quality connection that comes forward when the two are allowed to fuse and move as one?

Let us pick another quality. Perhaps we feel that if we allow passion, we will lose all peace. A passionate life is not an easy one, it is a life of strife. How can there be peace in it? This is a contemplation that could revolutionize how we connect to both peace and passion. Is peace a freeze on activity? Is it a constriction, a state of inertia, or a dead weight? If we make a feeling connection with peace, and bring the energy of passion into it, what happens? If we let ourselves be at peace with the natural ebb and flow of passion, what happens then? Can you sense the deepening empowerment and the relaxation into the field of pure potential?

Sometimes the quality conflict can be sneaky. For example, we might not feel able to allow passion, because we are just unable to feel it. We can be so caught in the quality of manifestation, that we are unable to allow the unmanifest source – which is the emptiness out of which passion arises. We make manifestation a condition of passion. In a way, we want the pudding to be proved before it is tasted. This patterning is quite common in our conditioning in which we are addicted to control. It effects our attitude to all qualities, as all of them arise spontaneously out of the unknown, out of the unmanifest.

So often, this controlling pattern means we want to know the way we are travelling before we have walked it; we want to know the way we will feel before we will feel it; we want to know that which is unknown before we will know it. We want to get a grip on the manifest form before we will allow the manifestation.

Of course, this critical difficulty with emptiness or dissolution will interfere with passion. We want passion so much, we despair at the lack of it, barring our own entry to the unmanifest field of pure possibility. Let us again quote David Bohm:

> *"Space is not empty. It is full, a plenum as opposed to a vacuum, and is the ground for the existence of everything, including ourselves. The universe is not separate from this cosmic sea of energy."*

In the reunion between qualities through split fragments of the psyche, a powerful healing process is occurring. Sometimes, a third quality will come forward as a needed bridge. For example, the quality of authority could come forward as a resource in the negotiation between truth and passion. Or the quality of wisdom could come forward in the negotiation between passion and innocence. All qualities are of service in the liberation of all other qualities. The dance of true nature will spontaneously attune to the needs of the here and now, especially when the quality of passion is allowed back into the family.

What qualities appear on your horizon as obstructions when you consider the transmission of passion through your body, heart, and mind?

Nondual Passion

17. I'VE GOT TO SPLIT

Passion as trauma and the healing of trauma

"I believe not only that trauma is curable, but that the healing process can be a catalyst for profound awakening - a portal opening to emotional and genuine spiritual transformation."

PETER LEVINE

You will already have gathered the enormous healing power of passion in its transformational effect in turning suffering to service, through the arousal of visceral energy pivoted to meet the greater need of the whole. When we perceive trauma through the window of passion, we begin to touch the cutting edge of human evolution, where the orchestra of biological and psychological responses turn from incapacitation to resilience and wisdom.

A dispassionate investigation sees trauma as an affliction of the psyche in which the personality undergoes events and becomes broken, wounded, or damaged. This damage is tragic and hard to heal, especially when the trauma is deemed complex – not a one-time acute event, not even a chronic repetition of events over time, but a complicated interaction of wounds that cannot be separated from who the person actually is.

Conventional trauma treatment is often to do with restoring functionality, which addresses a symptomatic level which is secondary to the core wound. In harder cases, this means that we call on medication or incarceration, or both, as a blanket way to save some functionality. Yet often medication has an effect on the psyche like the carpet bombing of a village. It indiscriminately disables the personality, making it dependent on outer authority for navigation, regulation, clarity, direction, and stimulation. It is a kind of chemotherapy that uses the combined forces of boredom and addiction to mute the scream of pain. Medication can buy time for healing to happen, but it cannot heal us. There is not, nor will there ever be, a pill to get rid of trauma.

As long as practitioners view the client as a definable personality, which can be further defined through diagnosis and psychiatric labels, the healing of trauma will seem impossible. This is especially the case where practitioners have little resilience themselves in the darker areas of experience - when they are afraid to go there. Then, they can join forces with the client in the agenda to get rid of the horror as soon as possible – and if not to get rid of it, then to deny, distract or numb it. When the practitioners are themselves limited in their freedom to experience suffering, they can easily become co-facilitators of abuse. One previous psychologist of a client of mine who had suffered severe marital abuse, even threatened her that if she had murderous feelings toward her ex-husband, she would have to be arrested.

Practitioners seek to help the client let go and move on. Yet often, the core trauma is not in what we hold onto, but in that which we never agreed to own. How is it to be told to let go of something that you have been trying to get rid of for your whole life? How can you let go of that which you refuse to hold? How can therapy be effective when the practitioner is keen to repeat the bypass of pain that has become part of the cycle of trauma?

For conventional psychology, the trauma is in the event that happened. This is how they come to the definitions of acute, chronic, and complex. It is based on physical events. But when we look deeply into trauma, we see that the field of trauma is not the event, it is in our naturalness, our true nature. The environment of trauma, the background of trauma, the place where trauma happens, and the most daunting association of the trauma is always a quality of our naturalness.

Nondual Passion

If our body has been wounded, the field of trauma is not the knife. Nor is it the cutting or the site of the wound. The field of trauma is the body in its open sensitivity, a moment before the knife struck. This is the field of trauma, and this exposed, unexpecting naturalness becomes the greatest trigger of alarm.

To move this into Nondual Therapy, the field of trauma is not the event, the shock, or the bad or sad feeling that happened. The field of trauma is in the qualities of true nature. For example, it is in our naturalness, purity, innocence, or trust. This means that the environmental triggers that set off the alarm bells of danger, will not be the circumstances of distress, for distress becomes habitual, but in the unwitting sensitivity of our naturalness.

In the moment of traumatic shock, the powerful energy of the nondual quality gets associated with the traumatic effect. For example, the energy of the nondual quality of helplessness gets fused with the energy of violation; or the energy of care gets fused with the energy of abuse. Later, when we feel helpless, we already sense violation. Helplessness becomes a suffering. The feeling vibrations have been associated and they carry a tremendous charge. This charge is not destined to be bad but is unconditional vitality. It is the charge of passion. In the words of pioneer of Somatic Experiencing Dr. Peter Levine: "The paradox of trauma is that it has both the power to destroy and the power to transform and resurrect." [8]

218

Our traumatized, reflexive conclusion is to never, ever, let ourselves be defenseless in that quality again. We blame the quality for the trauma. We blame the purity for the rape; the innocence for the theft; the trust for the betrayal; and the passion for the disaster. True nature is no longer felt as a field of endless nurture, but a minefield full of potential danger.

Trauma splits parts of our experience away from the integrated whole. This happens because traumatic experience is dissonant, and incompatible with ordinary consensual reality. Energetically, traumatic dimensions form alternative centers of the psyche. Trauma is a sub-dimension of the psyche - a vortex, spiraling around its own center of perception. When we are in it, it has a tremendous sense of truth, purpose, and reality about it, but it is out of connection with the whole.

We might be going about our normal day, feeling connected and relaxed, when a young but flirtatious teenage girl comes into the office. We notice how our male colleagues respond to her, one makes a joke about sex, virgins, and angels. Suddenly, it is as if we are psychically in suspension. Their voices are distant, and we are now falling, falling through the trauma tunnel into our alternative reality. From here, our workmates are incestuous predators. We feel like mucking them up completely. We are seething with malicious intent. We would be ready to throw both teenager and colleagues into the abyss.

Nondual Passion

Something feels impossible. We move in slow motion, as cold as ice. Deep inside, we want to die or kill or both. What was it that really ruptured our norms in this sequence of events? Was it that our colleagues are assholes, as they have always been? Or was it the exposure of the purity, freshness and vulnerability that showed up in the form of a teenager, catching us unawares?

Traumas in the field of passion can show up in diverse areas pertaining to our primal physical manifestation. For example, trauma involving the quality of passion can be found in the breathtaking shock of injustice; in the mind-swimming dread of being falsely accused; in the terror of destroying others; or in a brutal sense of being banished. As one client said: "If I let my true passion out, then people will die."

As passion surges upward from the dark, formless source which is prior to the personality, trauma in the field of passion can also show up as a vast sense of distance from the world or from others. The trauma locks us in the shelter at the source of passion, which would be restful, except that it is pervaded with the stifling air of isolation – and a deep alienation from all forms of life. It is empty but it feels like we are eternally caught. It is deadly but dreadfully alive, negating yet wild in the firing sparks of short fuses and ruptured wiring.

When we are traumatized in our passion, we hide ourselves away, sheltering behind psychopaths and fantasizing all forms of bypass. We conform with religiosity, obligation, and duty, but then find ourselves in a voiceless scream of rebellion from within the dust of the stone-like state of our soul. We try to release the screams of hell through substance abuse, but find the flames just rise higher, growing hotter with each day of our very boring yet horribly stressful lives.

Three factors show up with every trauma: true nature; shock and judgmental mind. The judgmental mind, as shown earlier, is deeply divisive, organizing reality into competing opposites. It is this nominally protective faculty that will state that passion is at cause of the trauma. Slicing the world into good and bad, it will make the passion bad, energetically associating it with all the evil sourced in the pain of the experience.

Passion gets demonized as a coping strategy to avoid the repetition of the pain. Yet in this demonization of passion, we have also robbed ourselves of the primal resource of nondual healing – the vitality and purpose behind our broken personality and within our unique manifestation as a living history.

To reclaim our connection with passion we need to own our natural authority at the center of all that we experience. In the words of Bessel van der Kolk:

"The challenge of recovery is to reestablish ownership of your body and your mind — of your self. This means feeling free to know what you know and to feel what you feel without becoming overwhelmed, enraged, ashamed, or collapsed." [9]

Healing trauma in the area of passion involves moving above this faculty of judgmental mind, and the unwinding of divisive beliefs. We need to move beyond the extremes and find middle ground. For this, the practitioner needs to enter an immediacy of experience with the client as the traumatic effect shows up in the here and now. This will not be the oft-told story of events, as much as the real-time psychophysical vibrations of the energetic field of passion.

The healing intensity is facilitated through consciousness, which at the same time, through the intensity of the here and now, can bring perspectives of infinity (boundless space to let the pain move, even when it feels unbearable), and eternity (unlimited time to come to relaxation and to gradually let the process unfold). This is so important, because the very mechanism of trauma is to get rid of the difficult experience. If we try to heal it away fast, under performance pressure of time and space, we are reinforcing that mechanism. We are rejecting the rejected parts of ourselves and again demonizing the passion.

What we are doing as practitioners in this time, is holding energetic space for the full spectrum of passion, no matter how it might manifest. This can be creative or destructive, a rage for life, or a wish for death. It can show up as sinister or fiercely free. It can threaten us with suicide and insist with violence on self-despair. The precise and unique passage of pain will claim superiority and will be grandiose. It will dictate the truth and humiliate the wayfarer. It will accuse you of failing to release it and condemn you to hell.

As practitioners, we stay as the dark and undifferentiated emptiness at the core of passion, as the innocence of passion, the service of passion and the destiny of compassion. We stay as the dark silence out of which all passion resounds, facilitating the energy to rise up in the client. The person's unique passion is never pitted against the rest, but is allowed to rise, together with all that has gone down, because of all that has gone down, and irrespective of all that has gone down.

Change occurs with a relaxation of stress responses, and a repatterning of the nerve system from the expectation of danger to the anticipation of reward. Perspectives starts to shift as attitudes loosen and transform. The sense of reward further relaxes the psyche, allowing it to open to greater flows of passion. It is a kind of soul retrieval, embodiment, or reincarnation of quality.

Nondual Passion

With passion, as with all nondual qualities, the healing configuration is one of and-and, not either-or. The quality of passion is no longer sacrificed on the altar of personal survival. Our client is allowed to be passionate about the transmission of their deeper truth. In this, they learn that it is safe to open the psyche to its own source, and to experience the power and purpose of their lives. Nobody dies, nothing terrible happens, nothing gets compromised. Soon, they will be deeply enjoying it.

The flow of information through the body, mind and soul is restored, as trauma fulfills its evolutionary purpose and becomes resilience, a resilience which is of direct service to the whole.

Georgi Y. Johnson

18. OPPOSITE SEX

Sexuality and the unifying principle of passion

"The Tantric sages tell us that our in-breath and out-breath actually mirror the divine creative gesture. With the inhalation, we draw into our own center, our own being. With the exhalation, we expand outward into the world."

SALLY KEMPTON

While the subject of nondual sexuality merits its own book; we must touch on it in this book on passion. This is because sexual trauma has hijacked passion, as if passion were exclusively sexual. In the same way, the difficulties we have with passion distort the naturalness of our sexuality. Like sexuality, passion is often feared as wild, destructive, and dangerous to the wellbeing of the whole. Passion is often only acceptable where there is a way to sanitize it of sexual vibration. But when passion has been won at the expense of such a brokerage, the sexual will to live will show up sooner or later, sometimes with a vengeance.

While the word sex means separation into gender, it also means reunion. Every one of us passed into physical life through the sexual field of our parents. In this creative meeting position, we were conceived. We are an expression of physical unity. This atmospheric layer of sexual reunion is indelibly part of the psychic core of each of us. It has its own life. Reunion or wholeness is a core drive of passion that surpasses survival instincts; for all separation must dissolve to find unity. In the words of Carl Jung:

> *"Passion that goes beyond the natural measure of love ultimately aims at the mystery of becoming whole, and this is why one feels, when he has fallen passionately in love, that becoming one with the other person is the only worthwhile goal of one's life."*[10]

We are aware that to even venture the topic of sexuality is like entering a battlefield naked between warring archetypes, stereotypes, and gender types. The theme of sexuality rattles all contractions and can inflate our complexes, for example, around love, care, power, esteem, or authority. Can you sense the helplessness which is there?

Sexuality is primal to creation, purpose, and passion. Through the forces of sexuality, we are conceived. Through its rhythms we are transformed. It is a doorway to wholeness in which the active and receptive dance in living stillness. It is the drive within incarnation, contraction, manifestation, and unconditional release. A natural expression of the law of attraction, our sexuality is inseparable from our passion, just as our passion is inseparable from our sense of purpose.

We are so injured in our relationship with sexuality that there is little consensus as to what it is. Some would reduce it to the act of intercourse. But at what stage does intercourse begin? With ejaculation? Would that mean that lesbian love making is not sexual? With penetration? Erotic touch? Erotic thought? Erotic feeling? Where would we draw the line? Is our sexuality to be allocated to certain body parts – so called erogenous zones – while excluding non-erotic parts? Is that realistic? Is our sexuality even primarily physical?

Our sexuality is a perceptive faculty; it is a system of sensory perception. Just as we have a sense of sight, touch, or smell, we also have a sexual sense. This sexual sense is far from originating in fantasy or thought, it is at once spiritual and physiological. It is as physical as our sense of smell. It has a sensory depth which expresses the unity behind all the other senses. The sense of sight, touch, smell, taste, and hearing will easily serve our sexual sense, as will the sense of balance and the sense of gravity (ever felt the sensation of falling into an erotic zone?). It includes intimacy, freshness, familiarity, beauty and belonging and it has the power to clear blocks in connectivity, inside and outside of ourselves. Sadly, many of us have been numbed in this core navigational faculty of consciousness. We have been blinded, muted, deafened and deprived of the direct flow of sensory information.

Our sexual sense is an integral, indispensable, primal, navigational organ of consciousness, which we have dumbed down and stigmatized beyond belief. We do this out of the fear of suffering and our mental agenda to avoid it.

Division bells

At the core of creation, there is division. The one expresses itself as a division into two. The one is not lost, but it is multiplying. The word "Sex" reflects this division, where one whole becomes two sections, a pair of complementary opposites in perfect polarity. It is a primal split, a trauma, the original rupture, perhaps like a shell breaking open. Yet each separate form is made of layers of the whole. Separated through expansion into polarity, all the parts remain connected through the inside source of origination. They are inseparable, as each contains the other. Through the separation into the manifold, the law of sexual attraction comes into play on the wings of love, the longing for peace and the passion for life. The very rupture of space between one form and the next leads to the bliss of touch, a bliss for which physical life is hardwired.

Within the bliss of touch there is the pain of separation. Without the space of separation, there can be no bliss. Without distance, there can be no reunion.

Therefore, the sexual dimension is one in which we find the greatest pleasure and also the most unbearable agony. It is home to astounding existential beauty but also the daunting certainty of loss. Beyond pleasure and pain, it vibrates with this causeless, unpossessable bliss. We fly to it, cry from it, and die into it. It takes us beyond the in-flow and out-flow of our breathing, to the continuum behind both. In visceral, sentient, biochemical form, sexuality presents the awe of a new universe, but also the horror at the ruptures of birth and death.

"It is strange that the older texts only know sexus. The modern meaning of sectiō 'division' suggests that sec/xus might derive from secāre 'to sever', but the morphology remains unclear: does sexus go back to an s-present *sek-s- 'to cut up', or was it derived from a form *sek-s- of the putative s-stem underlying secus?"
[Michiel de Vaan, "Etymological Dictionary of Latin and the other Italic Languages," Leiden, 2008]

Nondual Passion

In the sexual dimension, eternity meets the moment and infinity vibrates through the intimate quivers of form.

From a longing deep within the existential darkness of our essence, a passion begins to stir, a passion for life. It is held through unity; an arousal occurs in which threads of experience divide and differentiate. The more our consciousness can touch and release each moment, the faster the flow of bliss. This bliss is a healing factor, destroying limitation and conceiving fresh form. It is part of our inbuilt formula for physical, psychological, and spiritual wellbeing.

As this arousal moves through the pelvic area, arising from unconscious to subtle awareness, and diving back into the ocean of the unconscious, new forms of experience are born. That creative threshold is where form emerges, but it is also the origin of pain, due to onset of separation, and loss. It is a field of impermanence, and we are challenged to allow the ocean spray of it. Wherever we are wounded, or conditioned by trauma, wherever we have an agenda, we try to possess and control the breaking waves of sensation. We try to grasp the bliss and avoid the suffering.

This control leads to the pulsing of contractions – layers of restraint and restriction on experience. Wherever there is constriction of space, we suffer pressure. Wherever there is constriction of time, we suffer emergency. This pressure seeks release. In sexuality, the released energy will have the flavor of the movement of repression – for example, an erotic flavor of prohibition, shame, naughtiness, or the taboo.

Our sexuality is unconditional and ultimately untrainable. Sexual healing involves permission for these energies to be released in the way they were compressed – in a state of fusion with the suffering. Given the space of expression, each resonance can find its place again. Shame is shame, it is not married to sexuality. Shame becomes erotic, until the erotic is released from shame. The sense of wrongness is the energetic residue of judgmental mind, it is not integral to our sensual aliveness. With the gift of space, sexuality becomes revealed in its true nature, which is not evil, but blissful, healing, regenerative, transformative and of service to the wellbeing of us all.

To return to center, behind habits of grasping and aversion, our sexuality is a visceral ally. As vitality moves through the body, bliss separates into aspects of pain and pleasure, harmony and dissonance, presence, and absence, in an unfolding, imploding, creative flow of experience. Wherever we have been restricted, there is the possibility of release. Wherever we have become caught in form, our sexuality challenges us to liberate the attachment and to release the vibration to the whole. Wherever we believe we are limited, pain will come forward as a signal to return to the deeper layers of existential freedom.

Somatic, reflexive attitudes to suffering are formed. Difficulties with suffering are mirrored in our sexuality, and again in our relationship with passion. Our sexual resistance shows up in areas of numbness where we are unresponsive. It also shows up in addictive patterns, such as the compulsion to objectify, to cling to performance technique, or to discharge as soon as possible (to act out sexually as a means of getting rid of the discomfort of sexual desire).

As bliss divides into pleasure and pain, we demand the pleasure while trying to avoid the pain. To avoid pain, we must numb our sensitivity. When we numb our sensitivity, we close the sensual apparatus, opening it only according to learned conditions. These conditions vastly undermine trust in ourselves as the experiential center. We reach outside of ourselves for instruction and safety on when we should open and when not. The instructions we receive from external authorities are disconnected from the here and now. The result can be that our pelvis turns one way while our head turns the other. At a certain stage, the struggle leads to a numbing down and distancing of the sexual field away from the body, through fantasy or projection. The association of sexual arousal with danger leads us to dissociate from tactile experience. When this becomes habitual and reflexive, we can find the psyche normalized in a ruptured state.

Within this consensual normalization of our state of sexual dissociation, we suffer awful numbness in the place of natural, embodied awe.

Where our sexuality is conditioned, so is our passion. The chief conditioning element is the threat of suffering and death, a threat often exploited by religious power structures. Mainstream religious sects have been rigorous and rigid around the theme of sexual purity. But this purity has been all about getting rid of sexuality, which in a patriarchal structure means getting rid of women as the opposite sex. They have sectioned women, dictated dress codes, dogmatized coping strategies, silenced half the world's population and shamed and blamed all naturalness. This gender sectarianism fueled by fear and pain is a far cry from the service toward the wellbeing of the whole that religion pretends.

Sexual purity has been confused with sexual negation in the form of abstinence. Abstinence could lead to a deeper contemplation and to sexual self-realization, however, it has often been used as a form of control. The subjugation of tender dimensions of sensual aliveness already wounded by prohibition can create a violent, shaming attitude toward others – an epidemic of sexual condemnation.

Closure of the sexual sense also has the effect of closing the other senses, for example, consider a religious devotee who will not look at a woman, for fear of confrontation with his own sexuality. What happens to his sense of sight? It is a whole sensory lockdown in the name of a god the father.

Sexual dogmatism has had a devastating effect on our sexual consciousness. We have learned that our sexual intuition and instincts are unsafe. We have been taught to repress and oppress one another, rather than to support our aliveness and celebrate togetherness. Sexual arbitration, manipulation and control is not only in the prohibition of our sexuality, it is also in the forcing of it. We feel obliged to deliver sexuality in order to be "OK". This forcing of sexuality also has consequences to our naturalness, causing us to pretend, and disconnecting us from the deeper agony of violation that blocks access to the soft and honest depths of our spontaneous sexuality.

Energetic coping reflexes show up as cycles of sexual boredom, followed by rebellious outbreaks in which the unbearable voltage seeks safe release. This can show up as the acting out of addictive patterns in the world, reaching into pornographic abstraction for relief, but rarely reaching the sense of fulfillment. These patterns hang on scaffolds of sexual stereotypes and consensual, senseless norms. They have a deep resemblance to the areas of boredom and addiction written about in relation to passion in Chapters 12 and 13.

So what is sexual purity, really?

Imagine a married couple making love. Under obligation of the marriage contract, their sexual expression has become habitual, uninspired, cozy, nostalgic, but somewhat dead. Yet that same obligation says they must engage sexually x times a week to be "OK". To push through, each one fantasizes about something forbidden. Arousal happens. It is all within the law, but the direct sensory experience has been deflected into the mind. Their consciousness has been lifted out of the body into a dream world, each one of them on their own trip. The very drive toward reunion and the deep rest in togetherness shows up as the opposite – two carcasses strewn together, from which the souls have long since strayed, overcast by generations of marital loneliness. There is at best a contractual misalignment, a raw, physical meeting position and warmth, and a functional status quo. The sexual beast is tamed.

This is just a harmless and common example of the loss of connection with sexual purity. Healing would look something like forgiveness and allowance of that energy of erotic deviance, within the purity of the shared sexual sense. They could risk talking about their experience. They could give permission to the absence of desire, and sense what is there in the space. Through exploring and sharing the direct sexual sense, or lack of it, they have the possibility of immediate reunion on an embodied journey together. Also, we close our eyes to rest sometimes and deep sexual rest is natural, needed, and OK. Within this permission, sexuality can dance with passion and purpose through all the layers if life.

Sexual purity has nothing to do being loyal, obeying laws or staying within social contracts. It has everything to do with the purity of physical sensation in the here and now, including the purity of the experience of arousal and the experience of surrender into the boundless dark precincts of peace, rest and rejuvenation found at the core of the sexual dimension. It is connected with the freedom to like or dislike, to desire or repulse, to be carried by a wave, or to be alive in stillness. It is about the freedom to experience an unfiltered psychospiritual, intimately physical aliveness. It is about the release of the belief in separation through the emancipated field of pure experience.

It is sometimes when we do something sexually that we disconnect from our sexuality. The doing can be an attempt to discharge sexual power – a way to escape sexuality rather than to surrender within the experience of it. It is these explosive and forbidden acts, these shocks and betrayals that have built up such a field of pain around sexuality, reinforcing our fear of it. Yet these explosions are the effect of a bottleneck, a ruptured field of experience where sexuality has been denied, not the effect of the allowance of experience. The voltage gets too high, and the pressure overwhelms the lie, and then with a psychosexual violence, we hurt people. These movements always demand a disconnection from the whole. The disconnected sexual energy, protests and perpetrates the disconnect by ignoring heart, mind, and environment. In naturalness, a free sexuality is in confluence with the wellbeing of heart and body. In wholeness, the awareness of pain to those around us regulates sexual desire. Those who are sexually overactive are paradoxically often undersexed – their sexual sensitivity is in a state of rupture and shut down.

The less we use our sexual sense, the more we become afraid, and the more we attempt to control others. As we lose connection with what is actually attractive or alluring to us, we increasingly put the authority on the outside, getting horribly entangled with the fear of rejection which in the sexual dimension can feel like child murder. This is how tender, young, responsive, raw, and alive our sexual sensitivity can be. Where it is wounded, it either goes dead, or howls with agony. We cannot deny or disguise such a fundamental part of our makeup for long. When we do, it controls us from behind the vigilant flashlight of consciousness.

It can be hard to return to the sexual perceptive center, yet this is a deep movement of loyalty toward who we truly are. Each movement into sexual purity can unlock the opportunity for passion to flow. Sexual fear and contraction can close the door on our passion and purpose, but it can also be that which releases it. Just as we do not need a particular object for us to open our eyes and see, we do not need a partner for us to open our sexual sense and experience the bliss of the physical miracle.

Just as we dread suffering, we fear sexuality, and we distrust passion. Just as we have been conformed, brutalized, and humiliated in our gender, so will we meet obstructions to the free flow of passion. For women, this can be in the difficulty to take time and space for expression, as if individual manifestation requires permission from others. For men it can show up as the fear of domination, abuse, abandonment, and failure.

Passion opens the possibility of centering in our physical aliveness, as the sensory headquarters of all experience. The healing effects of this are many and far reaching. We have the chance to switch tracks from the flow of suffering, disempowerment, humiliation, conformity, and rejection, into the counter flow of healing, transformation, and service to the whole. We can let ourselves be moved from the layer of distraction and pain, to the deeper flow of true nature. Through passion, we become unique channels of the greatest resource, which is the source of all we are.

19. THE DEVIL YOU KNOW

Passion, the fear of evil and the evil in fear

"Whatever is done for love always occurs beyond good and evil."

FRIEDRICH NIETZSCHE

Somewhere along the way of the evolution of mind we have developed a compulsion to judge ourselves and others. This kind of compulsive moral judgement hijacks the natural judgmental faculty which is about measurement, spatial or temporal balance and navigation. It repurposes what is a mental support in mastering form, and uses it for the allocation of blame, the accusation of wrong, and the perception of evil.

The system of compulsive moral judgement has possessed our mental freedom, claiming an autonomous reality that can make it feel perilous to be human. Judgmentalism can seem structural to the psyche. The judgment between good and bad has a formational impact on our energetic state. We are in its throttle hold, and the prospect of moving beyond it can seem to threaten punishment, insanity, or death. So much of our personalities, our rapport with one another and our sense of belonging, can seem to depend on it. But it starves us of the spontaneous arising of our natural passion. Yet precisely because of this strangulation on passion, passion is the quality that has the powerful, embodied momentum toward wellbeing that can bring release from the monopoly of judgmental mind.

All the qualities of our true nature arise out of a dimension of being that is unconditional to the split between good and evil. The unconditional love that flows through us toward a child, for example, flows regardless of judgement of good or evil. The energy of peace is unconditional to the supposed split of good and evil, which is a state of war. The energy of truth also moves beyond judgement, if it were to split into the allocation of good and evil, it would not be truthfulness, but the abuse of truth.

The quality of passion also charges through the artificiality of judgment, moving through and beyond the energetic twin trap of good and evil. Yet passion is commonly associated with evil. Its freedom, strength, lawlessness, selfishness and seeming lack of care for protocol generates a nervousness around it. It threatens evil, and so is received as a form of evil. This conditioning can mean we reflexively deny, suppress, and ignore the passion arising in ourselves and others.

So, what is this evil that can persuade us to repress our passion? Is passion indeed evil? Perhaps.

When we endeavor a feeling inquiry into the nature of evil, we come upon pure pain. It is a pain so excruciating that it takes the breath away. Its potency burns out our defenses. It can feel more vital, essential, and real than all our ethics. It threatens to obliterate all the qualities of true nature. It monopolizes perception, engrossing experience. There is only this timeless, unchartered existential horror.

Yet although it threatens spiritual and existential annihilation, evil is impotent. It is the scream of pain that comes with the rupture of creation. Its greatest threat is the experience of its own vibration. This is a cosmic howl of pain – the primal suffering written about as an integral part of passion.

With a reflex to protect, the mind tries to grasp at whatever is deemed good and pleasurable, and to push away what is deemed bad and painful. Pleasure is tagged good, and pain is tagged evil. This is an energetic association. Our experience of pain now has a flavor of aversion. It is hated, despised, rejected. Pain becomes blended with the sense of hatred and even contempt. It gets associated with rejection and death. Born in the rupture of separation – a rupture in which bliss also emerged – this part of the creative experience is now demonized. It is pure evil, and we want only good.

Wherever we go to war for good, we propagate evil. When we perceive another as evil, we are sending them the frequency of pain. We are inflicting the primal pain of creation on their experience. It is a kind of moral violence through which we get an impermanent identity of being good or right. But when we espouse the blend of suffering, badness and contempt which is called evil, and channel it, we too are affected by it. In the words of Nietzsche: "If you stare into the abyss, the abyss stares back at you."

In our struggle to get rid of evil – in our aversion to evil – we add the energy of aversion – of hatred – to the pain. This aversion, contempt and hatred draws vitality from the primal vitality of pain. It seems more powerful than any mortal. It feels Satanic. Our worst fear is that we will discover this within ourselves. We dread that it is there, in the unknown precincts of the psyche. We cover ourselves up with protective layers of ego and strategies of righteous distraction. But we cannot hide it, as it forms a whole mist of wrongness around the psyche. Without location in space of time, it becomes formless and all-pervasive. We try so hard to be good, to be right, to be in the light, yet the darkness is spreading from within. We desperately need a scapegoat – a villain out there on whom to release this energy. We need an antichrist to give this inner evil a safe, external form – far away from us – a form that like us, is limited in time and space, and so a form that can be destroyed.

This villain can show up as a vindictive strain of a virus, or as an authority caught acting with cruelty and injustice. It can be classed as the opposite sex, or located in sexual predators, child-abusers, and narcissistic psychopaths. We find it on TV, in world leaders, and in terrorists. We desperately seek a space to safely let our sense of evil breathe. Only then do we get some relief from the inner distress of feeling wrong. All the time, we see ourselves as "good", righteous citizens.

The disempowerment of being right

As good people, we are victims of this evil world, victims of a perilous planet, and victims of a vindictive god that we do not believe in. As victims, we are always the "good" ones. Yet in our victimhood, we disown the suffering of the world, and the pain in the evil. We split the experience in the name of goodness, putting the badness on one side and the goodness on the other, so that we may banish the badness. As victims, we lie because we deny the same perpetrator that as victims, we depend on. For without an evil perpetrator, we cannot be a good victim. We depend on our perpetrators for our identity. In our righteous victimhood, we invade nations and occupy civilians with armies. In our victimhood, we pronounce death sentences on murderers – using murder to kill murder. We reject what is bad, and in this we propagate energetic toxins of badness and rejection. Each time we reject the badness, the pain of rejection within the badness gets more potent. We hate hatred, and in this we refuel hatred continuously. We are ashamed of our shame, and we feel bad because of it. We despise our jealousy and want to annihilate it because jealousy makes us bad. But now this jealousy is swelling with aversion, badness and the felt sense of annihilation. We dread that we might be evil at the core and that this should leak out. So that core pain is now clouded with dread, the dread of being seen, or felt, a dread of conscious revelation. Yet from the guts of ourselves, at the same time, we so much long to be seen as we truly are.

In our victimhood, we victimize ourselves again and again, disempowering the psyche and denying our own source. In the words of Albert Camus: "Virtue cannot separate itself from reality without becoming a principle of evil."

The plan to grasp the pleasure and get rid of the pain, to be good not evil, to be right not wrong, and to let evil be with "the other" is narcissistic because it is based on a deep belief in the primacy of the separate personality. It makes the personality – how it is seen, judged, adored, or rejected – the exclusive playing field of life. It glorifies and consolidates the notion of the separate self. The war between good and evil rests on the notion of separation from the whole. While separation is ultimately an illusion, the felt sense of separation – the suffering of rejection, miscommunication, neglect, abandonment and so on – is very real. It is a living vibration of pain. It is that same vibration that when we disown it, we call "evil". When we sense the selfishness within our separate agenda to be get rid of pain, we campaign still harder against the outer evil as this is blamed as the source of badness.

For a while, it can seem that the war against this outer evil is our deepest passion. But passion will liberate us also from the illusory split between good and evil. Passion is not caught in judgement which chooses between pairs of competing opposites based on like or dislike, right or wrong, good, and bad and the separate agenda of the separate self. As a vertical uprising, passion brings us to the center and to the middle way.

For and not against

The agenda to go to war against the "other", whether it be a disease, a political entity, or a concept, comes from adulterated passion. It is a wounded agenda hitching a ride on passion's fire. In its naturalness, passion moves on behalf of true nature, not against the many forms of affliction. It will fight for freedom, not against war. It will give voice to care, rather than mute the abandoned. It will bring power to love, compassion to anger, freedom to slavery, truth to dishonesty, and insight to confusion. As a quality of true nature, it relates to the true nature within all forms. Suffering is not something to be banished, it is part of the experiential fire which gives passion the vertical circulation that leads to compassion and wisdom and back to passion again.

When, on behalf of our agenda to be good and not bad, we project the sense of badness on the other, we leave a vacuum within. Each act of projection leaves a hollow, unoccupied space in the psyche. This absence of consciousness where energy has been disowned also has a physical effect – our sensitivity is numbed there – and without the flow of information through that area of the body or psyche, there is a lack of vitality. In those wounded parts of ourselves, where we have sent our inner pain to others in the projection of evil, we are disempowered. They become dispassionate, lacking real-time emotional aliveness. We feel hollow inside, and only the perception of evil in the other can stir something. Evil becomes a source of vitality and conscious awakening.

We become addicted to the belief in evil "out there", because only this evil awakens the sense of purpose. It gives us meaning, direction, and awakens a sense of power. We might believe we are crusading against all that is wrong, as righteous warriors, and yet we have become co-dependent. This evil world is the only thing that gives us identity and meaning. It becomes definitive. The same agenda to get rid of evil and be only good is now an agenda that is investing in evil, addicted to it, with devotion.

Beyond the pain we inflict on others when we project evil on them, we too begin to suffer horribly in the inner world. Often, we are most deeply hurt in those areas where we cannot express our qualities and talents. There is pain in the expression, and pain in early and repeating experiences of rejection.

For example, a boy who has a talent for sewing gets rejected by family and friends. The pain cuts him to the core, and something freezes over. It almost feels like his seeing is the cause of his parents' divorce and his father's later death. As an adult, a man comes into his office who loves to embroider. He is making a whole patchwork quilt in the lunch break. Our frustrated man-child is overcome with a sense of wrongness. It seems unfair and outrageous that his colleague is sewing in the workplace. It is not OK, he should be working, it is disrespectful and even abusive to the team. The colleague that is shamelessly sewing is seen as selfish, sociopathic, weird and offensive, lacking humanity. It annoys our man-child so much that he becomes obsessed. He wants to annihilate the activity in the present, future, and past. He fantasizes about torching the quilt. This leads to an erotic sight of himself under the quilt having passionate sex with the offending colleague's wife. Evil thoughts! The colleague must be dismissed.

The sense of evil can be triggered where others express those precious aspects of ourselves that have been shocked or forbidden – those areas where it feels our essence has been sacrificed to outer authority. It shows up as jealousy, rage, contempt, wishing ill, and distrust. Of course, we disown those unbearable feelings. They were done to us by the sociopathic "other". We are victims that do the "right" thing. These horrific sensations are because of the other. The other is the source of this sense of evil, which means that the other is evil.

In the name of the moral game

Tragically, in the name of moral game, we try to strangle the free expression of quality. We fight to repress our talents, gifts, beauty, and quality because this quality energy has been associated with pain. Because such quality vibrations are transpersonal (not caught in the personality), we fight them wherever they appear around us. We hurt ourselves and others, out of a terrorized refusal to come to life and beauty. We pass the evil between us, multiplying its effects, until the collective field becomes numb and dissociated. In the words of W.H. Auden: "Those to whom evil is done, do evil in return."

There is an innocence in the sinister pathology where the abused becomes the abuser, and the pain within it is calling out for a paradigm shift. Passion has the power to disrupt this terrible passing of the buck of pain, as passion is born of that same pain and is such a powerful affirmation and vehicle of true nature. Passion is the transformative fire that allows us to pass from one paradigm to another. With passion we can cross the river of suffering and reach the other side.

Each little move we make into the opening of the depth of the felt sense, regardless of the tired old war between good and evil, is instantly rewarded with wellbeing. This is because regardless of whether we sense pleasure or pain, goodness or evil, we are moving into the truth of our sensory nature. This freedom to feel which is at first fearsome, becomes freedom to be alive. We become empowered by direct experience, graced by beauty, endowed with insight, and blessed by a passion of care.

All our judgements flip over from the forbidden, to the permitted, revealing the liberation of the and-and, or the field of infinite possibility. In the words of Nietzsche: "The great epochs of our life are the occasions when we gain the courage to rebaptize our evil qualities as our best qualities."

These are the moments in which we step out of the judgmental, binary twin trap, and the world is revealed as a creative wonderland of multitextured potential. The linear story of our life dissolves into a masterpiece – which is the unique and magnificent opportunity to be a visceral co-creator of the human epoch in the unfolding here and now.

20. ONE & ALL

Passion, uniqueness and the collective

"I think the biggest disease the world suffers from in this day and age is the disease of people feeling unloved. I know that I can give love for a minute, for half an hour, for a day, for a month, but I can give. I am very happy to do that, I want to do that."

PRINCESS DIANA

Hidden behind words like "Everyone", "No-one", "People", and "The World", is a felt sense of a secret audience. This boundless audience is watching us, even in our private moments. Can you feel it? Do you feel yourself watched? Can you sense your audience? What kind of relationship do you have with it?

"It's complicated" – so goes the ambiguous relationship status on Facebook, which is an online epicenter of likes and dislikes, and virtual negotiation and strife between the individual and the collective.

In a way, we are all performers on a stage of consciousness. Moment by moment, we share our process with the whole. But this invisible audience does not disappear when we snap shut out laptop and roll over to sleep. It follows us into the neverland of dreams. It can feel like it is checking our progress, monitoring our development, or waiting for us to get to the point. Sometimes it is with us, but often it can feel against us. This audience has the power to approve of us or lynch us. It can appear as a boundless minefield of judgement in which human striving is reduced to a pursuit of acceptance and an avoidance of rejection. It is that same principle again, of going for the pleasure, and wanting to dump the pain. Only now, it's being played out through grandiose projections on the stage of "The World". The show must go on.

In this no man's land where there is a perceptive space to see and be seen, to listen and be heard, to feel and be felt, to touch and be touched, we have many wounds around manifestation. When passion arises through us and we begin to express quality energy directly into the world, the pain in these wounds can enter the foreground of conscious awareness.

Paradoxically, just when we are beginning to share the essential qualities of true nature with the whole, we can suffer the most intense loneliness, with the sense of being ignored, rejected, or even despised. Our audience can seem vindictive, intolerant, punishing, or loveless. It can feel like the very notion of our belonging in this collective energetic interchange is offensive. Sorry, this club is for men only. Look at the sign, blacks go to the back of the bus.

The apprehension of rejection can be even more personal, as these universal qualities are shining through the unique prism of our individual form. They are personal, and as they are sourced beyond the most private depths of ourselves, they are also intensely intimate.

Struggling with esteem, we feel worthless, and sometimes reach back into the world for proof of legitimacy through status, qualification, or certification. When we still feel unvalued, it can trigger a horrible pain of injustice. It is as if the world is stealing our birthright from us. It is so unfair. It is because it is a man's world, an English-speaking world, or a world of white privilege (choose your excuse).

All this could be revealed with a felt sense of an audience that is watching us with an attitude that directly reflects our personal wounds around passion. For some, the audience will be full of thieves, waiting to steal their ideas. For others, the audience will be uninterested, deliberately ignoring every word. Mostly, in the initial stages of the allowing of passion, the audience can be felt as hostile. This is a healing process in which that sense of hostility toward a vindictive world can move to compassion. It begins when we find the shared passion with our audience. We will find that shared passion when we begin to realize that this audience – this outer self-awareness - is a primary split made within our own psyche. Both the awareness on the inside and the awareness on the outside is our awareness. It is one awareness. This vast audience is our collective self, awakening as the whole.

Through the realization that outer is inner and inner is outer, we become further liberated in our feeling capacity. This is because we are no longer investing in the energy of denial that we use to partition experience. We move even more freely away from energetic habits of grasping and aversion based on mentally dictated divisions and awaken as the consciousness of wholeness or the wholeness of consciousness.

When the vibrations of the felt sense, such as feelings and emotions, are no longer labelled as only personal, we can recognize that they are at once personal and at the same time collective. The individual lives through the collective and the collective lives through the individual.

For example, the vibratory pain of separation that moves in us, is inseparable from the pain of separation in the whole human field. We can find oneness in the pain of separation. Even the deepest horror of abandonment is a collective horror, a collective dimension of suffering at the base of the one human psyche, at the same time that it is uniquely felt through us within the personal story.

The suffering in us is inseparable from the suffering in all humanity. This includes not only the suffering in which we are the victim, but also that in which we are the perpetrator. For example, the pain of being hated, and the pain of hating. Subject and object melt into a vibratory field that is here between us and within us.

When we are no longer compelled into reactivity toward vibrations of pain, we are free to experience them. This means we no longer get caught and entangled with vibrational atmospheres. For example, with the atmosphere of neglect: we are no longer compelled to identify with it, and to try and get rid of it by discharging it from the separate self. Where we were previously identified, and suffered being neglected, we have developed some resilience, some insight and access to healing resources. We deeply know what the suffering of neglect needs. This means that through passion, we have the chance to switch tracks, from suffering to service. Now, rather than shrinking within the suffering of neglect, we can channel a resource toward the suffering. In the case of neglect, this would often be a resource of care and freedom. This happens spontaneously but can be empowered through conscious alignment. We care because we are aware. We are free because we can open our hearts to the field of pain. These energies touch the field of neglect and the individuals caught within it. There is sentient benefit to the whole, including any leftover areas of neglect within our own psyches. The memory of neglect remains, but the sense of isolation, hopelessness and despair is relieved. Where there was conflict, there is now togetherness and a supportive presence of peace. Where there was separation between an individual and the whole, there is now a conscious affirmation of unbreakable, underlying unity.

We long for this unity, and where there is a free flow of passion, from the core of individuality out, we affirm this unity. The collective is elevated through the passion moving through the individual, and the whole morphic can begin healing through the sum of its parts.

When the collective is invective

This is all well, but what happens when the collective moves with denial, cruelty, violence, and rage, sweeping away the individual freedom and demanding another kind of unity? What is going on when the collective demands conformity toward a unified agenda, and tyrants and despots whip up what appears as the passion of the collective? What do we do in a groundswell of lynching, hate or war? Don't these collective evils show us just why we should avoid passion, lest it become collective? Shouldn't we then seek a separate self to save our souls? Shouldn't we then shun evil with the strength of morality and codes of ethics? Contrary to chapter 19 of this book, shouldn't we let ourselves judge, even if it means standing alone? Wouldn't we be justified in the deepest sociopathy?

From the micro to the macro, from individual to collective, this is the confusion that leads us to critical disempowerment. The manipulation of the collective field of disowned emotion, such as rage, hate and jealousy, is not passion but collective release. It is not a deep care and responsibility for suffering behind such movements, but a collective groundswell of emotional disenfranchisement.

Each time we refuse to acknowledge a resonance in our consciousness, out of fear of shame or blame, or just horrible discomfort, we avert our consciousness from it. The resonance does not disappear, it seethes beneath the threshold of consciousness. When we do that collectively, there are whole collective pools of rage, hatred, jealousy, and despair. These seek release in the safest possible way, without the risk of personal rejection from the herd. If we can find conditions where these emotions are framed as "good" and righteous, then releasing them can feel empowering. The collective field offers such a possibility.

When two or more are joined in a thought or an emotion, the emotional resonance becomes compelling. When a critical amount of people in a whole nation join up to a field of denial, righteous rage or hatred, many others will be energetically recruited. They will experience the same rage or hatred directly, as if it were their own. The collective becomes intensely personal and the old personal grievances are suddenly endorsed by the power of the collective. Collective emotional consensus can be compelling to the individual psyche, moving it beyond rationality, decency, and the natural ethics of the heart. The individual can become a channel through which disowned collective horrors are released.

The deepest taboos within these collectively disowned emotions, the darkest of the shadows, involve the active principle: the perpetrator. While we are all victims of cruelty, who would touch the perpetrating energic experience of being the abuser? Who can touch the sphere of suffering in which we find the inner sadist, or the unthinkable wrong? Wouldn't we rather murder ourselves through suicide, than admit to the inner murderer?

Our vulnerability to the sways and throes of collectively disowned emotion, and the manipulation of these energies by tyrants, is a direct result of our inner inability to take emotional responsibility. Where we do not own the resonance within our consciousness, that emotional energy becomes available for outer manipulation. The responsibility vacuums in the psyche are the entry points for psychopaths to engineer, control and possess us.

It is precisely because we cannot own the individual energy of sadism that the collective sadism possesses us. It is because of our disposal of the core pain of evil, that the outer evil enchants us. When we refuse to acknowledge our power, the active principle of perpetration, then we become servants to collective perpetration. We get emotionally driven by the psychospiritual disorder of the whole. This is a disorder in which we are limited to a psychology of war: it is kill or be killed; us or them; with us or against us, hero, or traitor.

Nothing on this planet, including the full force of collective man, has the power to separate us from our true nature, and the unity that is inherent to the source of all we are. As Krishnamurti said: "It is no measure of health to be well adjusted to a profoundly sick society."

To realize that the separate self is not ultimately real but is an expression of pain, is to move from the suffering of social conformity into the deeper, integral quality of the authority of true nature.

All over the mammalian brain, there are mirror neurons. These are the neurons of experiential resonance, sometimes called empathy neurons. When these neurons were first discovered, they were understood in physical terms. When the monkeys in a laboratory saw the scientist eating, the neurons fired as if the monkeys themselves were eating. The transpersonal resonance is there, and we respond to it. We experience what we witness, as if we were the one doing it. But this is not just physical, it is also emotional and spiritual.

We have the free possibility of blending in, first-hand with any experience in our environment. In any given moment, we could attune to an endless range of vibrations – from affliction in a tied-up dog, through to the sense of infinity in the sky above us. There is a natural freedom here, but we get caught where we have issues, where there is unfinished business, where there is conflict, or in those fields of resonance where we lose our compassion.

Where we lose our compassion, we also lose our freedom to attune. For example, if we believe everything is allowed except the death of children, then with the death of children we lose our compassion. The universe in that moment becomes evil, together with nature, god, and any ruling authority. We get caught in the field of resonance in such a way that we can no longer meet it. Our awareness forbids this pain because it is not allowed. But now we lost our attunement, so we resonate with this pain everywhere, in the death of a baby ant, a young tree, a news headline or a spoken word that even hints at it. When we see a propaganda poster showing a baby on a bayonet, we are ready to bomb whole cities of the enemy, including man, woman, and child. Through our core pain, on the strength of the collective, we became perpetrators of the very pain we refuse to feel.

Passion as the affirming flame

Passion is the alchemical quality through which the vitality of core pain expresses as an offering to the wellbeing of the whole. Passion gives us the power to stay as the resource of true nature, even amid emotional turbulence. Passion can offer a ferocious love and make us perpetrators of care. It dissipates fear and takes the vitality from any emotion and offers it in service to the collective wellbeing. The collective wellbeing is responsive, empowering us back, from the outside-in. The swell of collective emotion is undercut by a deeper current, arising from that inner dimension where the individual and the collective are one. The power of emotional consensus is dispelled through a deeper power – the pure quality of power – arising with the unnegotiable strength and wisdom of passion.

From this core dimension it is known that as a human being, I am every human being, and I am the one human being. In this, the greater depth, wisdom, power, and responsibility emerges. We become an affirming flame, as in the famous poem of W.H. Auden written at the outbreak of World War 2:

> *"Defenceless under the night*
> *Our world in stupor lies;*
> *Yet, dotted everywhere,*
> *Ironic points of light*
> *Flash out wherever the Just*
> *Exchange their messages:*
> *May I, composed like them*
> *Of Eros and of dust,*
> *Beleaguered by the same*
> *Negation and despair,*
> *Show an affirming flame."*

The resource of true nature offers source magic, that always outlasts the voodoo of tyrannical leaders. In the place of freedom of expression, passion offers freedom itself. In the place of the righteous rage, it offers the fire of truth. Beneath the urge to control, it offers the fearless power of all creation. Beyond the helpless energy of destruction, it brings existential energy that is indestructible. Beneath the compulsive urge to release emotion, it offers the unconditional release of unfettered, boundless awareness.

Nondual qualities are naturally expansive and are resonantly closer to true unity. Where emotional crisis can make the abyss a formless dimension of evil, true nature opens an unfettered dimension of emptiness which is a field of infinite creative possibility. Here, there are the core sufferings, including the suffering of evil. But also, here is boundless mercy, peace, freedom, love, and unity.

Both the individual story and the collective history lose authority as true passion emerges. This passion is sourced behind the suffering of time. Even death has no power over passion. It is sourced beyond the lostness of space. Even pure absence is passion's playground. The passion lives on, even after the body has lost separate form. Stirring in every expression of life, whatever its form, this passion offers the realization of unity, at the center-point of wisdom, and this allows the navigation of the collective malaise through a compassion that will liberate the whole.

Nondual Passion

21. IT'S IN THE BLOOD

Passion through the generations

"The collective unconscious contains the whole spiritual heritage of mankind's evolution born anew in the brain structure of every individual."

CARL JUNG

The materialist tendency of our era to try and physically control our wellbeing from the outside-in is reaching new extremes of intervention with the advent of genetic engineering, including gene splicing and cloning. It comes from that same agenda to get rid of suffering – to grasp pleasure and avoid pain – by interfering with our naturalness. The underlying assumption is that our naturalness is at best useless and that there is no deeper purpose within the natural expression of form. As long as that purpose is not known to the mind and not delivering immediate good effect, it is considered absent. There is arrogance in this approach. It assumes that what cannot be physically measured by us does not physically exist. It judges what should "be" and what should "not be" as an expression of form, on the basis of an antipathy to suffering.

Yet epigenetic afflictions to our natural expression often arise from energetic shock – from disruptions to the naturalness of our conscious wellbeing on a deeper level. This kind of intervention is reactive, operating from the dimension of effects on the dimension of effects, without treating the causal layer. It leaves the soul of the suffering behind. It takes the shell of the matter (as this can be grasped) and interferes with it, on the belief that there is nothing more than this.

Yet in the case of our genes, we know there is more – there are vast fields of evolving resonance, and vast mysteries that are yet to be unraveled. Even our understanding of what our genes actually are is in constant flux, and we have trouble honoring this.

Our living inheritance as human beings is found in the human genome. Here, deep within every cell of the body, there is life. Life is expressing through our heredity. Just as a song heard in the mind sounds different when sang, so does the expression of life through our genealogy take on living variety. In the same way that the singing does not negate the song, but adds a version of it, the unique expression of characteristics does not change the template. The template remains, and the manifesting song is a celebration of the template.

What is here in our DNA, in the templates within our cells, in the naturalness of our heritage? What information, intelligence or insight is available to us? Is it only physical? Or is there also experiential information, about the universe, evolution, wellbeing, and consciousness? Could it be that the whole "Akashic" library – the total of all experience from the C-Elegans worm to the human can be accessed right here, right now, through our genealogy?

Passion arises through the experience of unity. To sense unity, we need the quality of humility. As we admit that our brains, thoughts, attitudes, knowledge, and the whole history of science are inseparable from this repertoire of genetic expression, we begin to get a sense of where the real power lies. We begin to honor it. We open to the awe of the unknown and awaken as a field of unlimited possibility. That field of infinite possibility is found within every cell of the body.

Passion is part of our evolutionary momentum. At the core of this is the trauma of creation – the big bang of shock in which it all begins. The intensity of the shock demands the grace of space and time. This creative trauma has the mercy of endless time and infinite space to unfold through fields of experience. Through these fields of experience, trauma becomes resilience. Through it all, we are resourced by true nature and nondual qualities. These qualities are always accessible through the activating light of our consciousness. Pulled toward harmony and wellbeing, this generational healing and transmutation is our evolutionary purpose.

Through family lines, we carry aspects of this core pain. We choicelessly unfold differentiated vibrations of suffering on behalf of the whole. These are threads of individual heritage, where shock (awakening) and trauma (splitting) undergoes a process of healing through naturalness (true nature). When the cycle is complete, there is resilience, which allows space to rest back as the qualities of true nature. From here, the sense of agony perpetuating through conflict subsides into peace, as knowledge, insight and wisdom inform the physical systems on the deeper direction needed for the wellbeing of the whole.

Both trauma and resilience resonate through our genes and are passed from generation to generation. In the same way, our relationship to passion will be characterized through family lines. Passion is a core quality of physical manifestation, appearing at that pivotal moment where the instinct toward personal survival subsides into service for the good of the whole. As such, structures around passion reflect directly in the epigenetic patterns that effect the expression of our genes.

The subject of family trauma has gained popularity out of recent scientific evidence of altered gene expression through epigenetics. At the epigenetic layer (above the genes) a chemical process of methylation tags certain genes, inhibiting their expression. This is connected with all the different forms of survival – physical, emotional, and mental – and activates learned emotional associations around danger. Danger is about emergency, stress, and conscious awakening. The psychological physiology of epigenetics adds scientific insight to the felt sense of energetic inheritance and the embodied patterns of our individual purpose, as passed to us through the generations.

We know when we are moving in the evolutionary direction when the sense of purpose shows up, swiftly followed by the unconditional sense of fulfillment. Without rational cause, we get a feeling that we are the right person in the right place at the right time. This can follow chapters of family karma where it felt like the opposite, where we felt condemned as the wrong person at the wrong place at the wrong time. Between the family curse and the family blessing is the miracle of the living "you". When time, place and person align, evolution is happening.

Nondual Passion

Science is revealing that it is not only trauma that is in our blood, but also resilience.[11] This means we also inherit coping strategies, survival skills, talents, and patterns of wisdom. Without negating any form of experience, passion is the power at this nexus between trauma and resilience. All the way to our DNA, it is where our consciousness can make all the difference. Passion aptly fits the words of Mark Wolynn,[12] who is an expert in inherited trauma. It uses: "what was contracting us as the source of our expansion." The very agent of suffering is the principle of growth and manifestation. "Many of us don't realize that the trauma we are born to heal is also the seed of our expansion," adds Wolynn.

What is your family's relationship with suffering? Can you get a sense of what could fall away in terms of resistance, so that suffering could become passion, and passion manifestation?

Family units are sub-groups held together by biology and consensus. Part of the atmospheric consensus within family units is unconscious, inherited, and brought together through harmonic resonance in family lines. That means that if your father has certain attitudes around passion, then your mother probably has complementary attitudes. There will be areas of pure agreement, but also areas of dissonance. These patterns of harmony and dissonance around the theme of passion are being worked out in you. They will be in your blood, active now, or inactive waiting to be triggered by the right set of circumstances in the environment (for example, when you become a parent, when you reach a certain age, or when the world around you moves through a particular crisis).

Telltale signs of our inherited relationship with passion will be found in our family's attitude toward strangers. Is the stranger a danger? Is the focus on survival or revival?

Blocks in the flow of passion will show up at all of those interfaces between the family unit and the greater whole. What was our family's sense of belonging in society? What enemies were there? Did the family have a sense of purpose beyond the survival of the separate unit? What beliefs or agendas interfered with naturalness?

Sometimes families are broken. Here trauma will show up as deep divisions within the psyche, in the form of guilt structures and loyalty conflicts (spiraling around the qualities of innocence and trust). The fissures are deep because an either-or choice has been presented, between mother and father, when the child themselves can only ever be made of both. Yet out of the gap of the fissure, passion will be rising. Perhaps it will be destructive, angry, and afraid. But sooner or later it will bring a compassion that will heal and reveal a unity underlying all division.

Sometimes families are in states of slow decay. Here, are structures of emotional neglect, denial, vanity, tradition, and preservation. At a certain stage, the amount of available vitality gets so low that something collapses in illness or loss. It is the end of the line. Something new is coming out of the suddenly revealed emptiness.

Where there is a strong refusal to suffer or to own uncomfortable feelings, there will often be scapegoats. If there is not a pet "hate" on the outside, the scapegoat could be a family member, from the past or the present. This soul will be the receptacle of all the unwanted energies – such as the badness, sadness, destructiveness, or even evil. It is a particular kind of service, repeating the formula of Christ. The family's sacrificial lamb receives the accumulated vibrations of suffering, and without knowing it, releases back quality. For example, the child shamed in her sexuality will resonate back the pain of purity. It is rather like a flower that when crushed beneath the foot, that releases its essential fragrance. These individuals are well aligned to be path breakers in the family flow of passion. When the structure of victimhood collapses, the active principle arises with tremendous strength. Such scapegoats often appear as beacons of compassion, community leaders, healers, and true companions.

Whether or not we have children or grandchildren, we are a living legacy, and this is shared through the falling in love with the outsider. Out of this love, the next generation appears, teeming with the qualities of true nature. They are here as expressions of the evolutionary service of passion, bringing the elixir that turns patterns of pain to living resilience. We are all openly invited by this incoming generation into a rite of passage where suffering becomes the passion for life.

Nondual Passion

22. PANACEA

The passion elixir and nondual medicine

"The greatest evil is physical pain."

SAINT AUGUSTINE

Our wellbeing is a direct result of harmony between our true nature and all the vibrations of form, including mental, emotional, and physical. This harmony does not demand perfection, as nondual qualities are unconditional – they flow from beyond the limitations of time and space and are available regardless of our physical state. Harmony does not demand us to be perfectly healthy, but it does require a conscious spaciousness outside of the psyche.

For example, the spaciousness of pure awareness means we can be at peace with physical suffering. The peacefulness with imperfection, disease, pain, or physical affliction also opens the possibility of being at peace with where we experience health. That means we can also experience health, even when parts of us are sick. Peace has the power to move us out of the added conflict or competition between disease and health that often adds extra stress and despair. Again, the either-or, divisive programming of binary mind does us a disservice. The proof of living experience shows us that we are never completely healthy and never completely sick. We are a living interplay of both.

Another example is that we can experience wellbeing, regardless of how much of us is unwell and how much of us is well. Wellbeing is always here and in abundant supply, even in physical distress. It is always available. Wellbeing does not judge, but we exclude the sense of wellbeing by making it conditional on a standard of comfort or health. We try to control our health and wellbeing by putting conditions on the body, which is putting conditions on life. Wellbeing is literally "being well". It is about our true nature – the qualities of being – and our evolving realization that we are this, outside of cycles of suffering, birth, and death.

Check in for yourself if you feel this is true. When you are sick, do you love less? When you feel unwell, are you less yourself? When you have a virus, do you seem to lose direction? When you break a leg, are you ready to take care of others?

In most cases, the answer to all these questions will be yes – at first. A compromising physical event is a shock, a gamechanger. Something strikes home which is more real than our plans, ambitions, desires, and routines. We are shaken out of our habitual frame. There is an invitation to release conditions on our true nature and to awaken to what is really essential. In this, the habitual patterning of health and disease and disrupted, together with all the conditions we put on our wellbeing and on nondual qualities. When we confront our mortality, we begin to question what it is that we really came here for, what we really seek to experience, what is our purpose.

Becoming physically unwell crashes our normal patterns of acting out in the world and doing something to get what we want and opens up the possibility of change and evolution through the receptive principle. Suddenly, there is no escape from the physically alive questions held within the living body and held in our direct experience of being physically alive. We are crashing into passion as a first-hand, visceral, embodied experience. The pure science of being physically alive suddenly becomes very much applied.

Spinning around core helplessness, we get shifted from the active principle to the receptive. We are moved into the intimate dimension of need. We need to be seen in our suffering, and to feel love, care, and support. We all have difficulties in receptivity because we are helpless in it and risk becoming dependent. Many of us have spent decades being the active lover, caregiver, and doer and at first shun the notion of being on the vulnerable, receiving end.

What a bother to let the nurture of the other in! Who can trust this vibration of care, when it is followed so surely by the sense of loss? Who wants to be vulnerable to love, which loses patience and snaps at any moment? Who wants to be confronted with the demon of their own selfishness, when all their psyche finds safety in self-sacrifice?

There is stress in dependency, and physical distress brings this stress in the receptive side of ourselves to the foreground. The receptive side is where we are most complicated in our relationship with true nature. This is where we carry the wounds of the inner child. It is here that we were first shocked in our naturalness, becoming shaped by dose after dose of emotional dissonance. This is where the inner angel, master or guru was first exposed to the real politick of the wilderness of human suffering. When we are physically compromised, we are touched in that aching loneliness and isolated distress, from when we were on the receiving end of quality, as open-hearted, natural children, fresh, undefended, and helpless.

It is when we were young and dependent on receiving nurture that the qualities of true nature became experientially associated with pain. Here, where a parent abused us, the qualities of love, care and trust could now be fused with the energy of abuse. Where there was neglect, the quality of freedom could have been fused with abandonment. Where there was violence between our parents, unconditional wellbeing could become fused with an expectation of danger. When we are sick or in physical distress, this vulnerability in our relationship to true nature is awakened, bringing sentient echoes of the emotional distress at the core of the psyche, in the inner child. When we are sick, we can feel as helpless as children.

Our relationship with pain is somatically formed in childhood. This includes our coping strategies, attitudes, beliefs, and emotional responses to physical illness. In naturalness, we do not differentiate between physical and emotional pain. Pain is pain arising in a unified field of experience. The same brain areas light up with physical pain as with the pain of rejection, according to a 2003 study published in *Science*.[28] Although we try to divide ourselves into parts, there is no clear border between the physical dimension and the dimension of feelings and emotions: it is one field of experience.

How it expresses – physically, emotionally, or mentally – will depend on the environment. We opt for that dimension of manifestation that most effectively invites the qualities of true nature. For example, our scream of jealousy at the family dinner table is less likely to bring appreciation than a gut-gripping belly ache. It can feel safer to sweat out the toxic family shame with a fever where no pretense is required than to act out gross games or food fights. When we are physically impaired, there is less expectation of us to perform which can mean less stress and less emotional distress. We avoid the daunting prospect of becoming a failure or a disappointment to out tribe. Instead, we elect for the exemption of illness. For others it might be the other way around: there could be much more belonging possible through telling a heart-breaking story of bullying to our father than through throwing up on the kitchen floor. This also has consequences to wellbeing through all layers simultaneously. We live and learn.

Interdisciplinary pain

There is a highly responsive switch in the brain between emotional and physical response. This interpretation of distressing stimuli includes brain areas such as the hypothalamus, which simultaneously manages hormones, body temperature, daily physiological cycles, appetite, sexual behavior and our emotions. Signaling from the center will depend on overall connectivity and connectivity depends on the freedom of consciousness.

Where there is trauma, resistance, stress, and exhaustion, our connectivity gets reduced and we become less responsive in real time to what is needed for the wellbeing of the whole. Where we are caught in the agenda to avoid suffering, we lose information, connection, and physiological fluidity. We under-react, over-react, suffer isolation, and get caught in loops in which the system suffers its confusion on a secondary level, and again refuses the helplessness in the suffering.

Our pain expresses through varying layers through conditioned reflexes. We do not know we are doing this, and whether our immunological, hormonal and pain responses are sourced in the physical environment, in trauma or both, they are real. This brain switching between psychological and physical experience is programmed when we are children and can be reprogrammed when we are older. This reprogramming can occur through the fresh, rejuvenating, awakening of consciousness and vitality through the quality of passion.

The fields of psychoneuroimmunology and neuroplasticity are still in their infancy, but month by month, they reveal the holistic ingenuity of body-mind systems, and the impact they have on our physical health. All disciplines at the shifting frontiers of mind-body medicine require a paradigm shift from mechanistic, simplistic thinking. To advance, they require that the vibrational experience of the individual be the leader, acknowledging that feelings are both physically and mentally formative. They have a direct effect on, and express through, our state of health. We use our bodies to process stuff, and our tissues are working on our issues. The way we feel has a biochemical and neurological translation. Our emotions have a living physical manifestation, and where these are in conflict, we invite certain kinds of physical experience as a container to work the conflict out. Our bodies are of service in the deeper processes of our evolution, which involves the implicit and explicit unfolding of true nature. And it goes both ways. How we feel, the resonance of nondual qualities in the system, will give direction to the unfolding of healing in the body, offering templates of wellbeing, happiness and fulfillment, not only surviving but also thriving.

In Nondual Medicine, we go further, affirming that our ability to feel, our freedom to experience, and the liberation of consciousness, offer master-keys to the healing elixir of wellbeing. In this, passion offers a primary healing principle. Passion is the transformative energy through which our willingness to suffer as a service to the whole brings an alchemy of healing transformation.

Passion is the quality that has the power to switch the manifest form from destructive feedback loops into feedback loops of healing. Disorientation occurs where we fail to honor suffering. What doctor would presume to heal an affliction without first gaining insight into it? For the individual, who is the first authority on the sense of wellbeing, this insight into the nature of suffering requires that the suffering be felt. To feel a feeling or to allow a physical sensation, does not mean we get trapped in it, quite the opposite. The freedom to suffer brings freedom to suffering.

Through experience, the system gains information. Within this information is the need, and when we follow the need, the healing happens. When our suffering is held as the formula for healing, the nature of our experience changes, as our whole physiology and our consciousness becomes pivoted toward the wellbeing of the whole. This shift entirely depends on our attitude toward suffering, an attitude we are born with and which first unfolds in childhood. Is suffering a punishment? Is suffering happening because we have no value. Do we suffer because we are wrong and don't belong? Does our physical suffering even matter?

Between 1995 and 1997, the CDC-Kaiser Permanente Adverse Childhood Experiences (ACE) Study[13] conducted one of the largest investigations into the connection between childhood suffering and later-life health and wellbeing. The results were revolutionary, showing that the higher your ACE score, the higher the risk of long-term health problems. Childhood suffering was strongly associated with adulthood high-risk health behaviors including the full range of addictions, and was directly correlated with ill-health including depression, heart disease, cancer, chronic lung disease and shortened lifespan. A score of four or more adverse childhood experiences was associated with a 700 percent increase in alcoholism, a doubling of cancer diagnosis, and a four-fold increase in emphysema. Initially published in the American Journal of Preventive Medicine, the ACE study also uncovered increased risks in heart disease, stroke, and diabetes.

The ACE study establishes a proven link between psychological suffering and physical disease. Yet it is often taken as a means to screen high-risk individuals, and to try and stop child abuse and neglect through the education of parents. We are not yet fully awakening to the deeper implications: that whether we look at physical, emotional, or psychological wellbeing, we are called to invest in the healing of trauma.

To heal trauma, we need to move toward affliction not away from it. We cannot heal a rupture in the psyche with a psychiatric drug, we can only numb the stress of it. To address where we are traumatized, we need to be free and supported to experience the suffering in it and to offer this experience to the resilience of the whole. If we do not address it through the deeper opening of the heart today, our hospitals will be addressing it through the breakdown of public health in the future. Remember, passion is the quality at the tipping point where trauma becomes resilience. This is also the case physically. When passion moves through us, through the unique expression of our gifts, talents and qualities, the whole physical entity vibrates toward wellbeing.

The whole ACE study is based on lack. We can see in its methodology the tremendous confusion and disturbance to the whole psychophysiology when we are disconnected from the qualities of care, love, peace, authority, power, and compassion. It shows us the ticking bombs of disease that were planted when we were shocked in our naturalness, and the lifetime of stressful associations woven into our attempts to relax and open to life.

Above all, it shows us where we lost our passion, where purpose drained out of experience due to pure sentient dissonance, where the senses dulled and we retracted from life, no longer connected and no longer even wanting to belong. Even though on the face of things we might have still been functioning, our energy source was stress and counter stress. Within this stolen vitality, disconnected and unable to process the deeper pain for lack of resource in the environment, the cells of the body become depressed, undercharged, and dulled in receptivity.

The body is a processor of experience as much as the brain. Each time we become physically sick, there is the opportunity to rewire our relationship to suffering, which is our relationship to being alive. In the healing crisis, we have the chance to shift gear in repeating cycles of psychophysical suffering. The whole is devoted to the wellbeing of the body, just as the true healing of the body, brings formulas for the healing of the whole. This movement is all about passion.

To unlock the healing principle, which is passion, we take a step that moves beyond cleaving to individual survival. In our determination to be of service to the whole, to follow the sense of purpose, we move beyond the fear of death. In so many healing stories, there is this vital junction. The individual arrives at a position where they are ready to die in the disease. They lose hope. In this moment, they look into the dark night of despair, devoid of all purpose. But through their consciousness, through the existential gaze into absence, a deeper sense of purpose spontaneously begins to stir, as if out of the core of consciousness itself. In this arousal, there is an inspiration and empowerment to make this suffering or this death mean something. Experience finds purpose as a service to the whole. Some start to journal what remains of their time. Others share existential insights and peace. In many cases, this has led to remission of chronic disease, and to a vast expansion of true nature, with insight following insight. There is a kind of liberation in life. For the remainder of their time, people live well, and they die well too. There is suffering, but the pain no longer holds them. There is death, but the fear of it no longer restricts them. They are held in a wellbeing which is far greater.

Something to live for

In her book Radical Remission, Surviving Cancer Against All the Odds,[14] Dr. Kelly A. Turner, an expert in the field of integrative oncology, reports on nine factors that are at play where there is a remission from cancer in the absence of conventional medicine or after conventional medicine has failed. The factors are: dietary change; herbal remedies and supplements; individual authority; intuition; release of suppressed emotion (agreement to suffer); increase of "positive" emotion (agreement to resource true nature); deepening of spiritual connection (moving beyond the separate self); and strong reasons for living (purpose). Taken together, all these factors touch aspects of passion described in this book.

In the reclaiming of the authority of our own direct experience, within a wider, intuitive spiritual context, we allow the interplay of nondual qualities with both negative and positive emotions and states. In this we open our senses and life begins to make sense. We find a deeper sense of purpose, which orientates us toward the greater wellbeing of the whole. It is healing beyond survival – a release into the intimate yet unconditional dimension of the living, in which resistance is no longer the taskmaster of consciousness.

A fundamental part of every healing process is the movement beyond the fear of death, not in the sense of not having that very natural fear, but in the sense of being free within the fear, while accepting death as a universal principle which is inseparable from all forms of life. This movement beyond personal survival is the key moment where alchemy occurs, and the fear of suffering becomes the fuel of passion.

When we are free within fear, there is the possibility for fear to be experienced as bliss. In the words of one of this century's greatest pioneers in psychoneuroimmunology, Dr. Candace Pert, whose books include The Molecules of Emotion:[15]

> *"My research over the last 30 years has led me to this conclusion: we're actually "hardwired" for bliss – both physical and divine. By hardwired, I mean that we have major endorphin pathways that lead from the back of the brain to the frontal cortex, where we have the most opiate receptors: the cellular binding sites for endorphins... We really all are one. When you start to get this, maybe even only on a subconscious level, I think you will start to experience more bliss."*

Bliss is a tremendous healing factor. The neurotransmitter associated with both bliss and reward is Anandamide and is named after "Ananda" which is Sanskrit for primal bliss. As we noted earlier, bliss comes forward when we move out of the parameters of pleasure and pain, and into pure experience. Anandamide has a direct impact on the state of our immune system – our immunological attunement to the here and now. Anandamide and the endocannabinoid have been cited as therapeutically relevant to cardiovascular disease,[16] and has been shown to have an alleviating effect on inflammatory disease.[17] In one study, Anandamide was linked to the inhibition of human breast cancer.[18] While this research has led to a rush for pharmacological interventions, it is possible to recognize that the experience of bliss – including sexual, sensual and spiritual – will awaken and multiply the neurotransmitter, just as when we receive happy news, the brain floods with happy chemicals.

It is a philosophical, scientific, and medical responsibility to recognize the true, psychospiritual causality of the healing process. When we allow bliss, bliss is naturally signaled and allowed throughout our neurological, immunological, endocrinological, psychosexual, and cellular systems. It is a natural uprising of healing and regulation. The only way to stop it is through interference, such as with attempts to control it, possess it, create it, engineer it, and separate it from the whole.

The bliss of pure experience is expansive, it is asking to be shared. It opens the senses and life begins to make sense. You can feel bliss at any moment, even right now, by lightly touching the skin surface of your cheek with tenderness and care. Let yourself receive the bliss of the physical sensation. Let the cells awaken where they are touched. Let the physical sensation of bliss spread around the body, wherever it needs to go, from cell to cell, without controlling it. There is a physical, psychological, and spiritual immediacy in bliss as it moves us into the powerful authority of living qualities in the here and now. Here, we access deeper value, and there is an awakening of the sense of purpose.

Purpose differs from agenda because purpose is pivoted toward the greater whole. In the past decade, a research team, led by psychologist Barbara Fredrickson of the University of North Carolina-Chapel Hill and Steven Cole, a professor of medicine at the University of California-Los Angeles showed how the sense of purpose has a direct effect on physical immunity. To do this, the scientists differentiated between hedonic happiness (characterized by material or bodily pleasures such as eating well or having sex) and eudaimonic happiness (deeper satisfaction from activities with a greater meaning or purpose, such as intellectual pursuits, social relationships or charity work). They found that the latter – that in which energy traverses the energetic boundaries of the separate self - has a direct positive effect on the immune system.[19][20] Such findings show us that the immune system, rather than being a function of defense and attack between self and "other" as it is often described, is much more a system of compassion, communication, engagement, and resolution. Our wellbeing is a result of a willingness to move into areas of experience, not a compulsion to resist them.

Both the sense of purpose and the sense of connection directly effects our physical health. There has been a wealth of research into the correlation between disease and loneliness, the number one suffering of the belief in the separate self.[21] Speaking during the first wave of the COVID-19 pandemic, neuroscientist Prof. Asya Rolls of the Technion in Israel explained:

> *"Neuronal pathways that are involved in socializing are actually also activating specific pathways in the immune system... There are even studies that show being connected to something – togetherness – correlates with a better ability to cope with viruses. Another thing that is correlated with the activity and effectiveness of the immune system is how much people have a sense of meaning or of a bigger goal."* [22]

When we open to the sense of purpose, there is a willingness to be of service. We offer the experience we are having to the process of the whole. What follows the movement of service is often the vibration of gratitude, both within us and from the outside. Gratitude is also a healing elixir. Scientists have shown that feelings of gratitude can rewire the brain, releasing fresh vitality through alleviating areas of stress and depression, and encouraging the alignment between mind and body.[23] It has been shown to effect cardiovascular health or the wellbeing of the heart.[24] The energy of gratitude signals our willingness to receive the healing resources of true nature. It is only when we open in receptivity, that we may be healed, and that they can penetrate and awaken within the depth of the physical experience. This is not just a mental attitude, but a physical permission given through tiny receptors in every cell of the body.

When we move from surviving to thriving, regardless of our physical condition, we take a step from fear to freedom. This movement, out of the patterns of stress and depression which are a reflexive survival response to trauma, and into an agreement to live regardless of conditions, is where passion plays its role.

From the physiology of survival, we reflexively grasp what we know, and we develop a traumatized dread of the unknown. This dread is biochemical. It has even been found that the painkiller Tylenol (Paracetamol) helps relieve this existential dread.[25] In reverse, it must then be possible to bring the vibrations of relaxation and spacious wellbeing to relieve such pain-disorders as migraines. How do we find that spaciousness if not with a pill?

Existential dread, or the terror of the unknown can switch, through a change in attitude toward suffering, to the sense of awe and wonder. In both we disappear, but in the first it is in a cloud of anticipated evil. In the second, it is in the pure humility of opening to the beauty of creation. The vibration of awe, especially the responsive, existential awe at the interface with nature, has been shown to have a direct healing effect on inflammatory diseases and immune system function.[26] With the sense of awe, existential dread is released as the suffering of the unknown becomes the celebration of the mysterious. Passion is a core quality that enables us to move from the horror of the unknown threat to the wonder at the magnificent and endless possibilities of being alive.

A key aspect in the transformation from suffering to passion, and from physical distress into physical wellbeing, is found in the placebo effect. The placebo effect has been diminished by scientific dogma to delegitimize much of the healing which is not yet understood. However, placebo is not a bogus result of wishful thinking, but a real phenomenon which is creating real problems for pharmaceutical drug trials. When people get better even on a placebo, it shows that there are deeper healing mechanisms at work than the drug at hand. The placebo effect involves a complex neurobiological reaction that includes everything from increases in feel-good neurotransmitters, like endorphins and dopamine, to greater activity in certain brain regions linked to moods, emotional reactions, and self-awareness. With the ritual of the medicine, the switch gets flipped, from suffering to healing, and this has been shown to literally save lives.

Nondual Passion

Positive or negative expectations (with placebo or nocebo effects) have a direct impact on our health. The patterning of this subtle strata of expectation echoes that early relationship with suffering we covered at the start of this chapter. With the placebo effect, we are opening the area where attitudes of consciousness – such an attitude of wellbeing, care, peace, or release affect our physical health. It is through the alchemy of passion, that the nocebo effect that could kill us (such as a medical prognosis of one month to live) can turn to a placebo effect that can unlock an unconditional psychophysiological love for life.

According to Prof. Rolls:

> *"We know that when people have this positive expectation there is a brain area called the reward system and this area is activated. We have shown how a brain activated by the reward system attacks bacteria in the blood of mice. Just by activating the brain, they were able to kill bacteria much more effectively. We also showed it also with tumors, we can reduce the size of the tumors by half."*[27]

Bliss, purpose, reward, and the sense of fulfilment are all partners of passion. Again, the deeper individual responsibility is in how we meet life – how we are ready to let ourselves directly experience being alive.

Do you recall how in Chapter 14, we explored the inward movement to the core of longing? We showed how by tracing our felt sense into the areas of lack, through the missing, we find the inner, living memory of what we have been searching for on the outside. In feeling the love which we long for, we experience the love, and the love expands through the lack or ubiquitous emptiness, radiating back out into the world. In the same way, we can begin to understand the power of placebo effects.

The felt sense of what we miss (the missed love, care, or freedom) is found at the core of our physical pain. When we touch it with our consciousness it awakens and resonates. Vibrating from the inside-out, it sends healing waves reverberating the sense of wellbeing and expressing as "positive" expectation. Love calling from the inside, repeats through all the layers of form, meeting love on the outside. The whole entity harmonizes with greater wellbeing.

When we open our senses, life makes sense. The shock behind stress shines with the light of awakening as areas of depression begin to melt into life. With senses open, we become channels of consciousness. Consciousness brings the field of infinite potential and unfettered quality. As the ultimate resource of the living, consciousness includes the potential for miracles. We reorient from conformity to historic states of disease, to actualization of the deeper resonance of true nature. True nature gets agency, our agency, as a power source in which all layers of form can happily find themselves.

Passion panacea

When passion moves through the psyche and the psyche transforms to express the purpose or deeper need within passion, there are tremendous healing effects, through body, mind, and soul. It brings us to the aliveness of the here and the now, in which anything is possible. The dread of being shocked in our naturalness, because anything terrible could happen in any moment, transforms to the wonder and miracle of our naturalness, which includes the pure possibility of healing transformation. *Anything could happen in any moment.* This releases the infinite possibilities of healing.

In the brain, when we break patterns or take on new activities, there are a flood of neuronal stem cells. These allow neuroplasticity, which is how the brain heals itself. Stem cells are the undifferentiated master keys of life. They are full of the potential for everything. They are points of living cellular light seeking purpose, of service to the greater need. This is the same in the body. When the pure vitality of passion arises out of the ancient, epigenetic need in our bones, through the muscles and tendons, into the blood, warming and awakening every organ, messages of healing are flashed out in all directions. Stem cells are generated to meet the needs of the here and now, awakening to the mistress of consciousness, as she lights up the body. These stem cells have life-saving potential are able to differentiate to carry the light of all the healing qualities of true nature.

Passion is that quality that brings consciousness to the place of unmet need, that area of pain or imbalance, where it lights up the invitation to healing and transformation. As the whole energetic field of the body elevates and orientates to a oneness with all life, the field of possibility becomes truly unrestricted. Passion lives through us, we are lived by passion, and we find that we are this passion, in the awesome unfolding of the miracle of life.

Nondual Passion

EPILOGUE: PASSION CALLING

The end is the beginning

"The presence of passion within you is the greatest gift you can receive. Treat it as a miracle."

WAYNE DYER

Far beyond a witch's child, deep within the emptiness, far from the withered spaces where forms fear to fall, deep at the bottomless source of silence, there is a rhythm. Will you listen?

There is a rhythm. It is here in the blinking of eyes. It is here in the lips, in the mouth, in the swallowing throat. It is here in the stillness and it is here in this wide-open space in which all dreams appear. It is here, in the flickering, fluctuating, creating light of being. It is the rhythm of your vision, the rhythm of you.

There is a rhythm. It is the rhythm of a beating heart, from the start of it all pacing the tempo of a whole symphony of somatic sensation. This visceral ensemble - your organs, your cells, your blood, tissue, and bones – is playing a music most divine. Deep in the tone of the moan in the bones, made of fertile dust of faraway homes, and stars exploded, laughing symphonies of angels, and arousing songs of longing and joy. Here, rocking in this rhythm, the whole conscious theatre resounds with the familiar nuance, fluence and confluence of love, flowing with this fugitive, fragile, forever-human felt sense.

There is a rhythm. It is in this era, this decade, this month, this day, this hour, this minute, this second, and this moment of your sacred power.

There is a rhythm. It is in the cycle of the moon and the turning of the wind. It is the cadence of your naturalness, pumping nurture and air to every living cell, pounding freshness, purity, and chance after chance of life.

There is a rhythm. It is the tempo of your learning, letting old skins fall away, discharging the needless, releasing the past, and letting loss rest behind the insurgent night.

There is a rhythm, that devolves the unused to the whole great, manifesting wheel of birth and death; creation and destruction; becoming and returning; contraction and expansion. There is a rhythm.

There is a rhythm, resounding with a cosmic pulse, propelling currents flowing as knowing rivers that slow through sheltered spaces where we take sanctuary in salvation, pooling meadows of peace, before exploring on through erotic valleys and crashing over mountains, shedding ecstatic torrents of care over healing, merciful mountains of bliss, and immutable unity.

There is a rhythm. It is the rhythm of the soul as it roams, where days and nights, and suffering and strife, and rites of passage and the one true home, remind us of the arching sense of wonder in our being here, alone.

There is a rhythm. It is the hallowed mantra of deeper purpose, each beat bringing the power to move, to open, to touch, and to release the sacred endeavor, whatever, whoever, wherever, forever.

There is a rhythm. The rhythm of your feet walking the earth. The drum beat of destiny; pulsing time, space, and speed to love you in this precise moment, right here, right now, at the epicenter of worlds without end within an endless universe.

There is a rhythm. It is the rolling, thundering, enchanting empowering sound of hearts beating together, in their daring, imperfect brilliance. There is a rhythm.

There is a rhythm. It is arousing the ardor in each thread of sensuous appearance, all swaying through time and space as an articulated, unbothered bliss penetrates even the shadowy places where children fear and dying men draw near. It is the rhythm of completion singing from a distant star clear as a nightingale at the core of forgetting.

There is a rhythm. It is the rhythm of a distant bell, a bell that rings only for you. It is the sound of your calling, your meaning, your presence. It is your pulsating purpose, calling you to awaken. It is you, calling.

There is a rhythm. It is the rhythm of passion, the rhythm of pain, the rhythm of love, the rhythm of bliss, the rhythm of life, and the rhythm of the most empowering peace.

Can you feel it?

###

Nondual Passion

GLOSSARY OF TERMS

Awareness

Perceptive window through which we sense resonance, atmospheres, presence. Sentience.

Being

Soul, individual presence, center of feeling awareness.

Brain

The physiological entity of the brain including neuronal networks and detectable energetic frequencies.

Consciousness

Perceptive window through which we control, direct, invest and disinvest in forms of experience.

Contraction

Energetic seizure or cramp associated with stress and reduced sensitivity.

Collective

Social fields, sum total of people, including collective mind, psyche and unconscious.

Emptiness

Perceptive window through which we perceive through changing configurations of time (transience) and space (impermanence).

Nondual Passion

Energy
All forms and phenomenon including physical and subtle matter, such as electromagnetic fields, light, and more.

Epigenetic
Heritable phenotype changes that do not involve alterations in the DNA sequence.

Experience
The totality of perceptive impressions – including mental, emotional, and physical.

Felt Sense
Our sensory ability to feel any kind of vibration.

Field
A particular area of resonance or information. See "Morphic Fields" as referred to by Rupert Sheldrake.

Form
A sub-unity which has properties of time, space and frequency.

Mind
An evolving intelligence and center of perception that receive and directs the flow of information, beyond the physical brain in the same way that our sense of sight is beyond the physical eyes.

Mirror Neurons
Brain cells that reacts both when a particular action is performed and when it is only observed. "The neural basis for empathy may be a system of mirror neurons"

Neuroplasticity

The ability of the brain to form and reorganize synaptic connections, especially in response to learning or experience or following injury.

Nonduality

"Not two" or "one undivided without a second". The realization that the dichotomy of I-other is not absolute.

Nocebo

A detrimental effect on health produced by psychological or psychosomatic factors such as negative expectations of treatment or prognosis.

Passion

A quality of consciousness characterized by empowerment, purpose, creativity, liberation, and service to the whole.

Placebo

The power of belief to positively impact medical outcomes.

Psyche

Energetic substance wherein the information, patterns and configurations accumulate as an individual sense of self.

Quality

True nature: a natural and spontaneous resonance of conscious awareness, such as innocence, purity, peace. Perceived through the sensory capacity: i.e. the sense of truth.

Nondual Passion

Quality Complex

The attempt to recreate a nondual quality in such a way that it seems it can be controlled. A quality complex indicates a trauma in the naturalness of the quality.

Quality Conflict

An apparent conflict between two or more qualities as if they cannot co-emerge. For example, a conflict between trust and love.

Resonance

The reinforcement or prolongation of sound by reflection from a surface or by the synchronous vibration of a neighboring object.

Separate Self

The illusion that each self is independently existing and ultimately separate from the whole.

Singularity

A point at which a function takes an infinite value, especially in space-time when matter is infinitely dense, as at the center of a black hole.

Source

The source of all phenomena, preceding, underlying and succeeding any phenomena. Primal origination of consciousness, life, and all form.

Stem Cell

A stem cell is a cell with the unique ability to develop into specialized cell types in the body.

Suffering
Receptive experience that is painful or uncomfortable.

Talent
Skills, gifts, know-how. An ability that comes easily.

Trauma
A rupture between the normative experience and an unpleasant, exceptional experience that it is not possible to integrate with the whole, and so gains a degree of separate autonomy.

True Nature
The source qualities of consciousness, prior to the physical conditioning of time and *space.*

Unified field
The underlying, omnipresent wholeness beneath all universes.

Universe
The farthest reaches of our knowledge, perception, and imagination. The outer whole.

Vibration
An oscillation of the parts of a fluid or an elastic solid whose equilibrium has been disturbed, such as an electromagnetic wave.

Zero distance
The tipping point between intimacy and blending as one.

Nondual Passion

REFERENCES

[1] Not I, Not other than I: The Life and Teachings of Russel Williams. Edited by Steve Taylor. ASIN: B010TZ9XLW

[2] Nondual Therapy: The Psychology of Awakening, by Georgi Y. Johnson ISBN: 978-1-912517-00-8

[3] Buddha at the Gas Pump interview with Prof. John Hagelin and Rick Archer, #213, January 13, 2014. https://batgap.com/john-hagelin-transcript/

[4] American Society of Addiction Medicine (ASAM)

[5] Natural Rest for Addiction, Scott Kiloby https://www.kiloby.com/scotts-teachings

[6] In the Realm of Hungry Ghosts: Close Encounters with Addiction by Gabor Maté, ISBN-13: 978-1556438806

[7] 1997 Think Different marketing campaign from Apple Computers

[8] In an Unspoken Voice, How the Body Releases Trauma and Restores Goodness, by Peter Levine, 2010, p.37. ISBN-13: 978-1556439438

[9] The Body Keeps the Score: Brain, Mind, and Body in the Healing of Trauma, Bessel van der Kolk MD. Paperback – September 8, 2015. ISBN-10: 0143127748

[10] Man and His Symbols, by C.G. Jung; Dell Publishing Co., Inc. (September 1, 1968)] ISBN-13: 978-0440351832

[11] Cadet JL. Epigenetics of Stress, Addiction, and Resilience: Therapeutic Implications. Mol Neurobiol. 2016 Jan;53(1):545-560. doi:

10.1007/s12035-014-9040-y. Epub 2014 Dec 11. PMID: 25502297; PMCID: PMC4703633.

[12] It Didn't Start with You: How Inherited Family Trauma Shapes Who We Are and How to End the Cycle by Mark Wolynn; 2017; ISBN-13: 978-1101980385.

[13] Relationship of Childhood Abuse and Household Dysfunction to Many of the Leading Causes of Death in Adults. The Adverse Childhood Experiences (ACE) Study. American Journal of Preventative Medicine, VOLUME 14, ISSUE 4, P245-258, MAY 01, 1998. Vincent J Felitti MD, FACP; Robert F Anda MD, MS; Dale Nordenberg MD; Valerie Edwards BA; Mary P Koss PhD; James S Marks MD, MPH. https://doi.org/10.1016/S0749-3797(98)00017-8

[14] Radical Remission: Surviving Cancer Against All Odds by Kelly A. Turner. HarperOne; 1st edition (March 18, 2014) ISBN-13: 978-0062268754

[15] Molecules of Emotion: The Science Behind Mind-Body Medicine, by Candace B. Pert. Simon & Schuster; 1 edition (February 17, 1999) ISBN-13: 978-0684846347

[16] Martín Giménez, V. M., Noriega, S. E., Kassuha, D. E., Fuentes, L. B., & Manucha, W. (2018). Anandamide and endocannabinoid system: an attractive therapeutic approach for cardiovascular disease. Therapeutic advances in cardiovascular disease, 12(7), 177–190. https://doi.org/10.1177/1753944718773690

[17] Chiurchiù V, Rapino C, Talamonti E, et al. Anandamide Suppresses Proinflammatory T Cell Responses In Vitro through Type-1 Cannabinoid Receptor-Mediated mTOR Inhibition in Human

Keratinocytes. J Immunol. 2016;197(9):3545-3553. doi:10.4049/jimmunol.1500546

[18] De Petrocellis, L., Melck, D., Palmisano, A., Bisogno, T., Laezza, C., Bifulco, M., & Di Marzo, V. (1998). The endogenous cannabinoid anandamide inhibits human breast cancer cell proliferation. Proceedings of the National Academy of Sciences of the United States of America, 95(14), 8375–8380. https://doi.org/10.1073/pnas.95.14.8375

[19] How Happiness Boosts the Immune System, by Jo Marchant, Nature Magazine, November 27, 2013 https://www.scientificamerican.com/article/how-happiness-boosts-the-immune-system

[20] Kaplin, A., & Anzaldi, L. (2015). New Movement in Neuroscience: A Purpose-Driven Life. Cerebrum: the Dana forum on brain science, 2015, 7.

[21] Social isolation, loneliness, and mortality; Andrew Steptoe, Aparna Shankar, Panayotes Demakakos, Jane Wardle; Proceedings of the National Academy of Sciences Apr 2013, 110 (15) 5797-5801; DOI: 10.1073/pnas.1219686110

[22] Prof. Asya Rolls, Webinar with the American Technion Society, 25 March 2020. https://www.youtube.com/watch?time_continue=4&v=ZkaSdbb--e4

[23] Decomposing Gratitude: Representation and Integration of Cognitive Antecedents of Gratitude in the Brain; Hongbo Yu, Xiaoxue Gao, Yuanyuan Zhou, Xiaolin Zhou; Journal of Neuroscience 23 May 2018, 38 (21) 4886-4898; DOI: 10.1523/JNEUROSCI.2944-17.2018

[24] Greater Good Magazine. Can Gratitude Be Good for Your Heart? By Paul J. Mills, Laura Redwine; October 25, 2017

[25] Can Tylenol Dissolve Feelings of Dread? By Maia Szalavitz, TIME Magazine, April 19, 2013, https://healthland.time.com/2013/04/19/tylenol-fights-fear-of-the-abyss/

[26] Stellar, J. E., John-Henderson, N., Anderson, C. L., Gordon, A. M., McNeil, G. D., & Keltner, D. (2015). Positive affect and markers of inflammation: Discrete positive emotions predict lower levels of inflammatory cytokines. Emotion, 15(2), 129–133. https://doi.org/10.1037/emo0000033

[27] Ben-Shaanan, T.L., Schiller, M., Azulay-Debby, H. et al. Modulation of anti-tumor immunity by the brain's reward system. Nat Commun 9, 2723 (2018). https://doi.org/10.1038/s41467-018-05283-5

[28] Does Rejection Hurt? An fMRI Study of Social Exclusion. 10 OCT 2003: 290-292. Rejection by other people in a social situation triggers brain activity resembling that produced by physical pain. https://science.sciencemag.org/content/302/5643/290

ABOUT THE AUTHOR

Georgi Y. Johnson graduated from Oxford University with a determination to explore the mysteries of perception through mind, heart, and body. Together with her partner Bart ten Berge she has an international teaching and healing practice in Nondual Therapy and Spiritual Psychology.

Georgi is author of several books, including I Am Here – Opening the Windows of Life & Beauty (a study of the nature of consciousness), and Nondual Therapy – The Psychology of Awakening.

All Georgi's teachings arise out of the realization of the primacy of resonant experience in the movement toward wellbeing, health and happiness. In this, her approach is radically holistic, working with the vibratory field of the felt sense as prior to physical, psychological can mental manifestations. Implicit in this is the liberation of consciousness from the inherited conditioning of beliefs. Georgi presently lives with her partner and seven children in Israel.

Georgi Y. Johnson

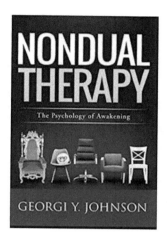

In Nondual Therapy- The Psychology of Awakening, Georgi Y. Johnson offers tools to release energetic contractions in the psyche, through the healing power of nondual qualities. This is a new healing modality, through which you'll discover:

- The evolutionary form of the human psyche.
- The transformative power of true nature.
- How to recognize and release energetic contractions.
- When to engage and when to "let go".
- How to manifest individuality in unity.

Nondual therapy is the master text of the nondual healing, series including a detailed compendium of nondual qualities and associated dualistic contractions.

CPSIA information can be obtained
at www.ICGtesting.com
Printed in the USA
LVHW011031100721
692282LV00008B/402